Voices of Diversity

Stories, Activities, and Resources for the Multicultural Classroom

Lori Langer de Ramírez

PEARSON

Merrill
Prentice Hall

Upper Saddle River, New Jersey
Columbus, Ohio

Library of Congress Cataloging-in-Publication Data

Langer de Ramirez, Lori.
  Voices of diversity : stories, activities and resources for the multicultural classroom / by Lori Langer de Ramirez.-- 1st ed.
    p. cm.
  Includes bibliographical references and index.
  ISBN 0-13-117886-5
  1. Multicultural educational--United States 2. Multicultural educational--United States--Activity programs. I. Title.
  LC1099.3.R345 2006
  370.117--dc22

                              2005023255

Vice President and Executive Publisher: Jeffery W. Johnson
Executive Editor: Debra A. Stollenwerk
Assistant Development Editor: Elisa Rogers
Editorial Assistant: Mary Morrill
Production Editor: Alexandrina Benedicto Wolf
Production Coordination: nSight
Design Coordinator: Diane C. Lorenzo
Cover Designer: Ali Mohrman
Production Manager: Susan W. Hannahs
Senior Marketing Manager: Darcy Betts Prybella
Marketing Coordinator: Bryan Mounts

This book was set in Garamond by Laserwords. It was printed and bound by R.R. Donnelley & Sons Company. The cover was printed by R.R. Donnelley & Sons Company.

Pearson Education Ltd.
Pearson Education Singapore Pte. Ltd.
Pearson Education Canada, Ltd.
Pearson Education—Japan

Pearson Education Australia Pty. Limited
Pearson Education North Asia Ltd.
Pearson Educación de Mexico, S.A. de C.V.
Pearson Education Malaysia Pte. Ltd.

10 9 8 7
ISBN 0-13-117886-5

Dedico esta labor a mi querido esposo, Ramón Orléy, por su amor, su optimismo y su fe.
To *m'hijo*, Nikolás, may he grow up in a world in which differences are not merely tolerated, but celebrated and embraced.

Preface

This text is designed for Multicultural Education or Curriculum and Instruction courses, or for inservice teachers who wish to expand their horizons concerning diversity and multiculturalism. For teachers at all levels of experience, this text will help open the door to deeper understanding of diversity issues and how to integrate this understanding into classroom practice.

As teachers, we are accustomed to being alone in our classroom with our students and our curricula. When we meet as teachers to discuss our practice, our focus almost always turns to our specific students or lessons. How often do we get the luxury of talking about our teaching, our own diversity, and ourselves? We spend too much time in isolation—alone in a room with three dozen or so children and confronted by issues that require hundreds of decisions each day. We rarely have the time to discuss our craft with our colleagues. It is thus no surprise to me that when teachers gather together, we inevitably talk about school. Despite the oft-quoted edict to "not talk shop" during social encounters, we will break the rules and talk about what's foremost in our minds—the classroom experience. The passion with which we discuss issues of importance to us—classroom incidents, our fears and hopes, our failures and successes—never ceases to amaze me. Given the time to share, we engage in a type of professional development that beats any that an administrator or school district might design. The need to communicate with other educators is so strong that it's often impossible to silence us once we begin to speak about the pedagogical issues that form the basis of our everyday classroom experience. Among the most important of these issues are the subtle elements of diversity, the many shades of racism that yet pervade the country, and the fine layers of one's own identity. How do teachers find the outlet for discussing these difficult issues?

Philosophical Framework

The concept of this book—a melding of theory and practice—is grounded firmly in Paulo Freire's notion of *conscientização*. This Portuguese term "refers to learning to perceive social, political, and economic contradictions, and to take action against the oppressive elements of reality" (Freire, 2003, Myra Bergman Ramos, translator's note, p. 35). It is the idea that equity issues and cultural imbalances must be first perceived so as to, as Greene (1988) so eloquently puts it, render the situation "problematic." On seeing a problem, in both Freire's and Greene's theories, the aim is to take action.

In *Pedagogy of the Oppressed*, Freire (2003) urges educators to form a praxis, a combination of reflection, dialogue, and action. Freire also highlights the need for a problem-based curriculum, cautioning teachers to avoid what he calls the "banking concept" of education. In this concept, the teacher is viewed as the "depositor" of knowledge into the head of the student. The student is seen as an empty vessel, a *tabula rasa*, and is assumed to have nothing to contribute to the educational process except for being a docile recipient of the teacher's "gift" of information. The teacher graciously imparts valuable knowledge to the student. The following cartoon illustrates this concept well:

A Brief History of Education

Note how the student begins his education with exuberance, with a vast store of his own knowledge. Throughout his education, teachers (depicted as disembodied arms) "organize" the boy's knowledge into more segmented parts, thus yielding a more regimented and thus more passive learner.

Freire's criticism reveals the discrimination and power issues inherent in such a pedagogy. The teacher is viewed as the *subject*, acting on a docile *object*. The teacher views the student as empty, thus reinforcing existing strength and power relationships in the classroom. Without the teacher's knowledge, it is mistakenly believed, there would be no learning.

Freire insists on the need to share information in a dialogical framework. He calls for an interaction to be defined as Teacher-Student and Student-Teacher. In this reconfiguration of the subject-object roles, teachers and students work together on a problem in a praxis in which reflection and action happen continuously. In this way, the curriculum is both shaped and reshaped through constant action and reflection on the subject at hand. The learning takes place, Freire would say, as problems are reflected on, talked about, and then worked on. I have designed this book on this same melding of thought, theory, and dialogue with activity and action.

The Role of Narrative in This Book

Teachers seem to learn best from each other in small groups and in informal discussions about practice. We tend to benefit from sharing practical ideas and suggestions. This sharing, in Freire's terminology, is the "serious reflection" of our practice that can lead to action and change. I have built this book around reflective narratives collected from parents, students, and teachers about real-life school-related incidents on a variety of themes of diversity and multiculturalism. By using authentic tales, I hope to encourage you, the reader, to think through each situation as if it were a case in your own school setting. As you read, ask yourself such questions as: "If I were in her shoes, what would I do?" or "How might I have handled that situation differently?" You might even find yourself saying, "That would never happen in my school!" or "I would never respond that way in my classroom." When you do, you may find it helpful to think about the differences and explore the idiosyncrasies of your school context in detail. Sometimes it is in viewing differences that we better understand our similarities.

It goes without saying that experiences in working through issues of diversity and multiculturalism vary from teacher to teacher. Some educators have worked extensively in their schools and communities to foster dialogue, establish inclusive school cultures, and change curricula. Others are just beginning to think about multicultural education and what it means for their own teaching. Stories are a particularly useful medium for meeting the needs of teachers at all points of this continuum. Teachers with more experience can dig deeper into the narratives and make connections to the research and theory offered in the suggested reading at the end of each chapter. Those of us just beginning this journey into exploring our own and our students' identities can begin by discussing the narratives as cases and may debate the actions taken by the narrators. Narratives are flexible and can be engaged on a variety of levels. Dewey (1966) describes education as a "continual reorganizing, reconstructing, [and] transforming experience" (p. 50).

Sharing stories related to teaching helps educators at all levels of experience to re-organize, reconstruct, and thus transform the craft of teaching.

Features of the Text

A Place to Begin

This book is meant to be used as a supplement to more thorough readings on the specific themes of diversity addressed in each chapter (race, language, gender, etc). Each chapter begins with a snapshot of its theme. This limited theoretical grounding provides you with background information for reading the narratives and participating in the activities and projects, and is a starting point for further reading (suggestions for that reading are provided at the end of each chapter).

We start each chapter by looking at a cartoon that reflects some aspect of the chapter topic. The following brief discussion provides you with a lens though which to view the subsequent narratives, allowing you to build a framework for thinking about the topic that combines both your own opinions and theory.

Before You Read

A prereading exercise prior to each narrative prompts you to start thinking about the topic addressed in the story. This exercise will lead you to explore preconceived notions you might have about the topic and to think about your own school context.

Narrative

Each chapter includes two narratives authored by a teacher, a student, or a parent. It is particularly important to note that the included narratives represent the primary shareholders in the educational system. In keeping with Freire's idea of praxis, this models an important theme in multiculturalism—the need to involve as many voices as possible. It is not always the teacher who reflects the "true" reality of the classroom situation; students and parents also have a chance to voice their thoughts on these important topics. This combination of voices also encourages you as teachers to think about ways in which you might open new lines of communication with these important shareholders in the educational endeavor. While you might have only virtual dialogues with these shareholders through the pages of this book, you will hopefully feel encouraged to seek out their flesh-and-blood counterparts in your individual school contexts for further conversations.

The stories included in this volume represent myriad views on different topics. It is imperative that you read them with a critical eye. The reactions, opinions, and descriptions contained herein are all those of individual teachers, parents, or students in specific contexts in particular times of their teaching, parenting, or educational careers. It is your task to read their stories and interact with them as if in an open and honest conversation with each narrator. Despite the fact that these stories are in print and housed in an educational text, you are not meant to swallow their content whole. Only through dissecting and analyzing the narratives can you effectively work through the issues that form their core. Take issue with the narratives; don't take them as gospel.

Questions to Consider

Following each narrative is a series of open-ended questions to explore the topic in general through the story details. These questions are simply a starting point for thinking deeply about the issues being presented. They can be used as writing prompts for your teaching journal, discussion starters for you and your colleagues, or simply as a stimulus for thinking about your own practice.

Whether you agree with the outcome of a particular narrative or oppose the actions the main character takes, try to be honest with your feelings and explore them in relation to your own teaching. By reacting to the actions of others in a supportive setting (whether that be in a class, a staff development session, or a small-group discussion), you will certainly gain a better understanding of your own tendencies in dealing with issues of diversity. And maybe, after reading these stories, this book will inspire you to write some of your own.

Project and Extension Activities

A series of short exercises and longer projects appears at the end of each chapter. These activities are meant to engage you in a more in-depth exploration of the theme of the chapter and provide an opportunity to investigate your feelings and ideas. Learning about and experiencing multiculturalism may be seen as a continuum. Some of us may be just beginning, with little or no experience of the issues discussed in this book. Others may have already taken courses in multicultural education, worked in diverse school settings, or done our own cultural explorations. The activities, like the narratives, vary in length and in level of difficulty. I encourage you to jump into the "multicultural stream" at a point that makes sense for you. If you consider yourself a novice, begin with some simpler activities. If you are interested in challenging yourself and have had the opportunity to think about and work on these issues in the past, try an activity that goes into more depth. It is up to your level of experience and your desire to stretch your understanding of the topic.

Cultural Exploration

A cultural exploration project follows each chapter's Project and Extension Activities. This exploration is designed to encourage deeper and more sustained interaction with a culture. Through it you might interview someone, visit a cultural or ethnic neighborhood, or read a novel. Whichever exploration you choose to undertake, it is important to be cognizant of the purpose of such activities: exploring another culture with an open mind and with the intention of discovering something new. It is imperative that you do not view any single exploration as definitive of a culture or group. Remember as you explore that this is one event, reading, perspective, or visit. It is always helpful to connect with a member of the group you are exploring to check your observations and get a deeper understanding of your perceptions and thoughts.

There are nine types of cultural explorations:

- Explore the Web—Visit and analyze websites and other Internet sites
- Explore teaching materials—Research and analyze multicultural content in textbooks and other didactic materials
- Explore literature—Read and analyze novels, young adult literature, and children's picturebooks
- Explore people—Meet and interview people from diverse backgrounds; discuss a variety of cultural experiences and different perspectives
- Explore neighborhoods—Visit a cultural neighborhood or area to gain a broader understanding of a cultural issue
- Explore other schools—Research and/or visit other school settings and observe different curricula in practice
- Explore your school—Analyze multicultural aspects of your own school setting
- Explore video—View and analyze a video on a topic of multiculturalism
- Explore film—View and analyze a film on a topic of multiculturalism

A useful framework for your exploration would include the following steps:

1. List your thoughts, concerns, and expectations prior to the experience. If possible, ground these thoughts in your own cultural identity and experiences.
2. Prepare yourself before exploring by speaking to members of the group, reading some background information, or doing some other form of preliminary research.
3. Write down your reactions and observations as you explore.
4. Synthesize and analyze your exploration by answering the question, "What did I learn about myself?"

Internet Connections

At the end of each chapter appears a description of important websites that correspond to that chapter's topic. These are excellent resources for finding out more about the issues addressed in each chapter.

References and Recommended Reading

This section contains bibliographic references for the books, articles, and other reading materials cited in the text, as well as sources for more information and further reading on the chapter topic.

Because of the book's linear format, its elements (theory, dialogue, and practice) are presented consecutively; ideally in praxis these elements interact, intersect, and re-form to create a neverending learning experience. Once you discuss a topic, you might call on new theory to answer new questions. Once you have asked new questions, new dialogue might emerge. Through this new dialogue, you may find yourself taking different actions and pursuing further activities. Thus, we may view the essential concept of the book as a diagram, where growth and action occur at the intersections:

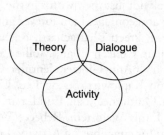

I hope that in reading this book, you will see yourself in many of the tales. My aim is to inspire you to share your own stories and, in doing so, make vital connections with your fellow educators and open lines of communication about the many complex issues surrounding multiculturalism and diversity.

Further reading

Bettelheim, B. (1975). *The Uses of Enchantment: The Meaning and Importance of Fairy Tales.* New York: Vintage.

Dewey, J. (1966). *Democracy and education.* New York: Free Press.

Freire, P. (1998). *Teachers as cultural workers: Letters to those who dare teach.* Boulder, CO: Westview Press.

Freire, P. (2003). *Pedagogy of the oppressed.* New York: Continuum.

Greene, M. (1988). *The dialectic of freedom.* New York: Teachers College Press.

Greene, M. (1993). Diversity and Inclusion: Toward a Curriculum for Human Beings. *Teachers College Record, 95*(2), 1–23.

Acknowledgments

Over the years, colleagues, friends, and students of my course "Teaching and Learning in the Multicultural Classroom" at Teachers College, Columbia University, contributed to this book not just their words in the forms of narrative and poetry, but also their honesty and courage. I am forever grateful to these individuals: Ehud Abadi, Noura Badawi, Preeti Bhattacharti, Rachel Brenan, Debra Burger, Ashley Capute, Charles Chan, Colleen Chan, Mollie Cura, Paula Davis, Johanna Fierman, Michelle Gannon, JoAnn Glotzer, Jennifer Grolemund, Milton Hernandez, Ranee Jaber, Aaron Kaplowitz, Seung Lee, Cici Liu, Patrick Maguire, Jerry Pavlon-Blum, Susan Quintyne, Joan Ruddiman, Meredith Serota-Alvaro, Hyun Jung (Drew) Song, Emily Weinstein, Rebecca Wolff, and Lauren Yokomizo. Thanks to Greg Bynum for contributing Activity 4 in Chapter 6 and to Paula Davis for contributing Activity 6 in Chapter 6.

Special thanks to Dr. Lin Goodwin, who first exposed me to many of the issues in this book. Her caring, wisdom, and insight influenced the structure and tone of this book in so many ways. And a very special thanks to Paige Braddock, creator of the *Jane's World* cartoons (*www.janesworld.com*), for her generosity and assistance in securing cartoon permissions.

Thanks to the following reviewers for their valuable feedback: Doug Fisher, San Diego State University; Kate Friesner, College of Santa Fe; Emiliano Gonzalez, University of St. Thomas; Nancy L. Hadaway, University of Texas, Arlington; Karen Embry Jenlink, Stephen F. Austin State University; John P. Kemppainen, University of North Florida; Kathleen Kreamelmeyer, Indiana University East; Patricia Ryan, Otterbein College; Gary M. Stiler, University of Southern Indiana; and Janeth B. Wahl, University of Nebraska, Lincoln.

I would also like to thank production editor Alex Wolf of Prentice Hall and Stephanie Levy of nSight, Inc., for their help in producing this book. I thank my copyeditor, Robert L. Marcum, for his exquisite editing. I especially thank Debbie Stollenwerk of Merrill/Prentice Hall for seeing the value in teacher stories and for having faith in my ability to share them with my teaching colleagues.

Lori Langer de Ramirez

About the Author

Lori Langer de Ramirez began her career as a teacher of Spanish, French, and ESL. She holds a master's degree in Applied Linguistics and a doctorate in Curriculum and Teaching from Teachers College, Columbia University. She is currently the chairperson of the ESL and World Language Department for Herricks Public Schools, New York, and served as an adjunct professor at Teachers College, Columbia University, where she taught "Teaching and Learning in the Multicultural Classroom."

She is the author of several Spanish-language books and texts, including *Mi abuela ya no está—Un cuento mexicano del Día de los Muertos* (Alcoi, Spain: Alfagrafic, 2000), a picturebook about the Day of the Dead, and *Cuéntame—Folklore y Fábulas* (New York: AMSCO, 1999), a folktale-based reader with activities. Lori has also contributed to many textbooks and written numerous articles about second-language pedagogy and methodology. Her most recent work involved developing an interactive website that offers teachers over 40 virtual picturebooks, pages of realia, links, and other curricular materials for teaching Spanish, French, and ESL (please visit at *http://www.miscositas.com*).

Lori has presented workshops at professional conferences both in the United States and internationally. She has been the recipient of several National Endowment for the Humanities grants to study in and develop lessons about Mexico, Colombia, and Senegal; an AATSP fellowship for graduate study; a grant from the Council for Basic Education; and most recently a Fulbright Award to India and Nepal. She received the Nelson Brooks Award for Excellence in the Teaching of Culture from the American Council on the Teaching of Foreign Languages. Her areas of research and curriculum development are folktales in the language classroom—especially stories from the oral tradition—and technology in language teaching.

Contents

6   Sexual Orientation   83

7   Religious Beliefs   105

8 Linguistic Diversity 123

9 Gender and Gender Roles 141

10 Learning (Dis) Abilities and Special Needs 157

11   Physical Abilities   173

Index   191

Introduction to the Diverse Classroom

CHAPTER

Cultural Programming Flowchart

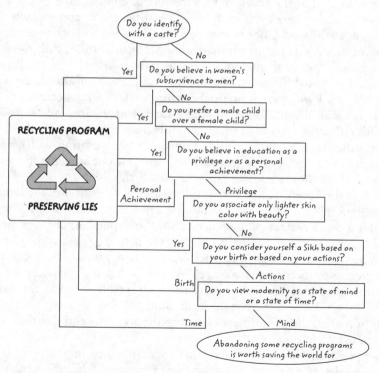

Do you identify with a caste?

No → Do you believe in women's subsurvience to men?

Yes

No → Do you prefer a male child over a female child?

Yes

No → Do you believe in education as a privilege or as a personal achievement?

Yes

RECYCLING PROGRAM

PRESERVING LIES

Personal Achievement

Privilege → Do you associate only lighter skin color with beauty?

No → Do you consider yourself a Sikh based on your birth or based on your actions?

Yes

Birth

Actions → Do you view modernity as a state of mind or a state of time?

Time

Mind → Abandoning some recycling programs is worth saving the world for

A Place to Begin

As teachers, many of us claim to not see differences in our students. We want to foster a state of equality in our classrooms, and may choose to focus on the similarities of our students rather than on their diversity. Somehow, one's sense of fairness is tied to this philosophy: treating students differently would not be providing children with equal educational opportunities. However, I propose that we *do* in fact treat kids differently every day in a multitude of ways—some overt and some covert.

We might begin by looking at ourselves as educators and as human beings. When we enter our classrooms, is it possible to leave our ethnicity, gender, and life experiences at the door? Getting in touch with our own identity is crucial for every educator.

I often hear teachers claim not to be very "cultural" or "interesting" in terms of their own diversity. These self-deprecating comments imply an inherent misunderstanding about the term *culture*. Being a member of the sociopolitical majority, white, heterosexual, Standard American English speakers may feel as if they have nothing to contribute to the conversation on multiculturalism. However, we must view the term *multicultural* in its broadest terms. We all carry with us into the classroom a vast store of cultural experiences and information. This "culture" that we bring is never neutral or apolitical. It frames the way we see the world, not to mention the educational experience. One way of thinking about this idea is through what McIntosh (1988) calls the "invisible knapsack." McIntosh uses this term to refer to a cache of privilege that whites in the United States possess unknowingly and that affords certain advantages. Here, I will reappropriate the term to refer to a collection of beliefs, ideas, tastes, and dispositions that we all carry with us into all facets of our lives. This culturally grounded collection influences the way in which we interact with others and view the world. Knowing what we bring with us in our "knapsack" will help us to understand how we view our students, how we interact with them, how we teach, and what we teach.

Look at the flowchart that begins this chapter. The artist uses the term "cultural programming" in the title. He poses a series of questions whose responses seem to indicate a certain cultural attitude. If the respondent answers the questions in a certain fashion, the artist feels that the person has been "programmed" and is a participant in the maintenance of a certain hegemony, or status quo. In this particular cartoon, the artist is referring to Sikh society and certain mores and norms that have long been considered acceptable, such as the belief in women's subservience to men or the association of lighter skin with beauty. The artist believes that these ideas have been recycled over time and that they serve to preserve lies.

Can you think of similar beliefs that are maintained in your own culture? Do you feel that you have been "culturally programmed?" If so, in what ways? If not, why not? What issues of diversity does this flowchart address? Which issues are most salient for you? Are there others that are not included that you would add to a flowchart for yourself? What might such a flowchart look like for you and for your culture(s)? What questions would it ask?

Before You Read

The first year of teaching can be challenging even for the best prepared of teachers. New teachers are confronted with issues of lesson planning, class pacing, and behavior management, along with more mundane concerns such as where to go for photocopies, which secretaries are the most helpful, and teacher's room etiquette. We rarely explore our own identity before stepping foot in our first classroom—there just doesn't seem to be time for such an investigation.

Think about your first teaching experience. What challenges did you face? What types of supports were in place for you during your first year? Who, if anyone, did you turn to for help and advice? Reflect on your first teaching position in relation to the cultures represented in your students. Were they similar or different? Did your students share your race? Ethnicity? Language? Socioeconomic status? What major and minor cultural differences existed between you and your students?

Expectations—A New Teacher's Story

I graduated college in December—a function of having transferred too often and not being able to finish the required courses the previous spring semester. For this reason, I believed that it would be impossible to find a suitable teaching position until the following September. Despite my fears, I mailed my short résumé out to school districts in my area in the hopes that there would be some way for me to get started in my chosen profession. I had been waiting so long—ever since I took that first seventh-grade Spanish class—and I knew that I wanted to be a Spanish teacher. I was eager to "get my feet wet" and get into a classroom—any classroom. I was surprised and thrilled when, in May, I was finally offered a job in a district known for its high poverty rates and at-risk students. "There are so many challenges connected to these factors. Would I be able to handle it?" I wondered. I didn't care . . . I was going to finally start teaching!

Hindsight, they say, is 20/20. I realize now that I should have asked some questions. Why was there an opening in May, when there was barely a month of school left? Who in their right mind would leave a class right before final exams? What happened to the teacher I was replacing? Needless to say, I didn't ask these questions, but rather skipped off to school one morning, wearing my new skirt suit, toting a new briefcase with new grade and plan books, and sporting a grin from ear to ear. I was actually going to start teaching. Sure, I had taught many lessons during my wonderful student teaching experiences, but this was different. This was going to be my own class.

When I arrived at the school that first morning, I went straight to my new classroom. As I walked through the halls approaching the room, I realized that the majority of the students were African American and the few adults I saw were white. I also noticed the decaying walls, chipped paint, and leaking ceilings. My classroom was filled with outdated textbooks, broken desks, decades-old maps, and a chipped blackboard with no chalk in sight. But there was no time to think about all this. The bell rang and my first day of teaching began.

My students filed into the classroom. One by one they eyed me up and down. Each kid took a seat and started doing what I imagine they had been doing for the past three weeks that they had been without their Spanish teacher—whatever they wanted to do. Some were throwing small wads of paper while others were chewing gum and blowing bubbles with a studied sense of blasé coolness. There were two smiling girls in the front row with notebooks in hand. I could tell that these girls were thrilled to have an actual teacher in the room. Their classmates weren't.

I cleared my throat and started to speak. "My name is Ms. Tobias. Here, I'll write it on the board for you. I will be your Spanish teacher for the rest of the year." My two eager beavers in the front row started scratching away in their notebooks. The rest of the class did not hear a word of my introduction. I tried to stop them by shouting over the din, to no avail. I was getting frustrated when I finally caught the attention of one girl sitting with her feet on the desk in front of her. I was relieved, thinking that I had reached another student. Slowly but surely, I thought, I would be able to reach them one by one until I had the whole class eating out of the palm of my hand!

"Hey!" my new student shouted to no one in particular. "What's this white bitch doing here?"

A few students snickered, several applauded, the two girls in the front looked appalled and apologetic. I must have looked like a deer caught in the headlights, because at first I didn't move. I stuttered in an attempt to say something, and then froze again. By the time I regained my composure, the girl who made the offensive comment was long gone from her seat. She had joined some friends in the back of the room and was happily chatting away about something or other.

I don't remember how I got through the class. I vaguely remember giving something more of a private tutorial to my two front-row students until the period ended and my students ran off to their next classes. I sat down and tried to figure out my next move. Along with the nasty comment from my pubescent pupil, I was reeling from the newness of the situation. This was my first experience in front of a class alone and I had no textbook, no curriculum, and no idea what to do. Over the course of the next few days, I tried to speak with my teaching colleagues, but they were little help. "Each teacher does his or her own thing, really," was the most common response to my request for curricular guidance. On day three, I knew it was time to see the principal.

The principal looked bothered by my presence in her office. "How's it going?" she asked begrudgingly.

"Well . . ." I tried not to sound too upset at first. After all, I was a new teacher and not eager to make waves. "I was wondering if I could get a copy of the textbook that the students have been using. And I want to get started preparing them for the final exam in June, but I have yet to see a copy of the test."

The principal looked at me blankly. "I see," she said, in a noncommittal tone, "Great! Great . . . . I'll work on that for you." She smiled slightly. "For now, I just want you to keep an eye on the kids. You know, make sure you don't lose any of them!" This was her attempt at a joke, but I wasn't laughing.

Something inside me made me strong, strong enough to say, "What you want is a babysitter, not a teacher."

She looked at me with that smile again. "Just make sure they don't fall out of the window!" With that, she ushered me out of her office and patted me on the back. "You'll do fine!" she said indifferently.

I went home and cried on that, my third night of teaching. What was I to do with the situation? I had students who I could not control and school leadership that had low expectations for those students. I was hired not to teach them Spanish necessarily, but just to keep them relatively safe while they were on school grounds. I wanted to teach . . . so I quit.

I still regret quitting that job. I ran away from the racial issues, the management problems, and the lack of administrative support. I ran away from an opportunity to learn from such a challenging situation. I expected to teach Spanish. My students expected a black teacher. My principal expected only that I control the students. What would you have expected?

Questions to Consider

1. The teacher in this story stepped into the classroom on the first day with some expectations of her own. Based on what you read, what might those expectations have been (i.e., what was in her "invisible knapsack")? What evidence in the story supports your hypotheses?
2. What could have instigated the disparaging comment from the student? Do you think that the teacher is correct in saying that the students expected a black teacher? What might make her feel this way?
3. It is obvious how the low socioeconomic status of the school affected the physical plant (leaky ceilings, peeling paint, old textbooks, etc.). How might it have affected the curriculum? The teachers? The students?
4. What might this teacher have done instead of quitting? What would you have done?
5. What do you think happened to the original teacher? How might the author have uncovered more information about the class and its history?
6. How could the conversation with the principal have gone differently? What could the narrator have said/done to get her needs met?

Identity and Power

Multicultural education has been a part of teaching and learning for several decades. Despite this fact, the idea of student and teacher identity and the issues of power that surround it are rare topics of discussion for teachers. Questions about race, religion, language, and sexual orientation are often avoided. We are more comfortable debating the newest textbook, the new style of teaching math, or the latest trend in youth literature rather than tackling the touchy subject of power in our classrooms. There is good reason for this. Given the overwhelming drive for political correctness in today's society, and especially in the educational system, many teachers worry about saying or doing "the wrong thing." By admitting to colleagues any insecurity about a racial issue, for example, teachers opens themselves up for possible criticism. Something offensive might be said, or an insensitive comment might reveal a certain level of ignorance, thus making a teacher feel vulnerable.

It is this very insecurity that helps to obscure these important issues. When we are afraid to ask for help, we are forced to handle diversity issues in the best way we know how. We rely on past experiences, which may or may not have been handled in an ideal manner. Furthermore, our own belief system plays an important role in deciphering the best way to handle the situation. It is at this point that the teacher's own identity comes into play.

We may glean a simple example of how cultural issues arise from a common classroom control situation. Teachers in the United States often tell students, "Look at me when I'm talking," and might even further insist that a student look them in the eye when being reprimanded. This request is culturally biased, though Americans seldom think of it in this way. Many simply think that it is "good manners" and do not give it much more thought. However, in many world cultures, children are prohibited from looking at their elders in the eye— it is considered *bad* manners to do so. Without realizing it, both teacher and student in this scenario are engaged in a culture clash. However, in the typical classroom, the teacher is the holder of power and the student is seen as subordinate. Given this relationship, then, the teacher by default is right and the student is wrong. In this way, the culture of the teacher—what the teacher considers to be polite—is considered "correct" and the dominant culture is perpetuated without the actors in the scenario really understanding the role that identity and power play in the school setting.

Consider educator Haim Ginott's (1993, pp. 15–16) comment on power in the classroom:

> I have come to a frightening conclusion.
> I am the decisive element in the classroom.
> It is my personal approach that creates the climate.
> It is my daily mood that makes the weather.
> As a teacher I possess tremendous power to make a child's life miserable or joyous.
> I can be a tool of torture or an instrument of inspiration.
> I can humiliate or humor, hurt or heal.

In all situations, it is my response that decides whether a crisis will be escalated or de-escalated, and a child humanized or de-humanized.

Our "invisible knapsacks," filled with cultural information, experiences, and beliefs, influence when and how and toward whom we wield this power.

 Internet Connection

Instituto Paulo Freire

The website of the Paulo Freire Institute offers courses, events, and a forum for discussion about education. One of its aims is to promote education that is "less ugly, less mean, less authoritarian, more democratic, more human." It also provides links to archives of Freire's writings and to new research endeavors.
http://www.paulofreire.org

Teacher Focus

An online forum for teachers to discuss all issues related to teaching. On this site, you can schedule chats with groups of people or simply join one of the many chat rooms organized by topic, such as "New Teachers," "Special Education," and "Teacher's Lounge." The site also contains links to resources and lesson plans.
http://www.teacherfocus.com

Teacher Stories of Curriculum Change

Sponsored by the Northwest Regional Educational Laboratory, this online book is downloadable as a PDF file (Note: you will need Acrobat Reader or another PDF reader to open the page.) It includes a collection of teacher stories with titles such as, "The Power of Reflection," "Navigating Sameness," and "Choosing The Road Less Traveled."
www.nwrel.org/lld/teacherstories.pdf

References and Recommended Reading

Borich, G. D. (2003). *Observation skills for effective teaching,* 4th ed. Upper Saddle River, NJ: Merrill-Prentice Hall.

Brandt, R. S. (Ed.). (2000). *Education in a new era.* Alexandria, VA: Association for Supervision and Curriculum Development.

Bruner, J. (1966). *Toward a theory of instruction.* Cambridge, MA: Harvard University Press.

Doll, W. E., (1993). *A post-modern perspective on curriculum.* New York: Teachers College Press.

Ginott, H. (1985). *Teacher and child.* New York: Collier.

Ibieta, G., & Orvell, M. (1996). *Inventing America: Readings in identity and culture.* New York: St. Martin's.

Kliebard, H. M. (1995). *The struggle for the American curriculum, 1893–1958.* New York: Routledge.

Lambert, L., Walker, D., Zimmerman, D. P., Cooper, J. E., Lambert, M. D., Gardner, M. E., & Slack, P. J. F. (1995). *The constructivist leader.* New York: Teachers College Press.

McIntosh, P. (1988). White Privilege: Unpacking the Invisible Knapsack. *Peace and Freedom* (July/August), 10–12.

Phillips Manke, M. (1997). *Classroom power relations: Understanding student–teacher interaction.* Mahwah, NJ: Lawrence Erlbaum Associates.

Postman, N., & Weingartner, C. (1969). *Teaching as a subversive activity.* New York: Delacorte.

Rand, M. K., & Shelton-Colangelo, S. (2003). *Voices of student teachers: Cases from the field,* 2nd ed. Upper Saddle River, NJ: Merrill-Prentice Hall.

What Is Multicultural Education?

A Place to Begin

So many of us have heard the term *multicultural education* as just one more example of educational jargon. As with much of our terminology, the phrase means more than its component parts. *Multicultural,* of course, means "having to do with a variety of cultures," and *education* implies some sort of information related teaching and curriculum. But the actual definition of the term and how it plays out in a given school or classroom can vary widely from context to context.

Multicultural education can be traced historically to the Civil Rights Movement during the 1960s in the United States. Following the turbulent period during which the nation's schools became desegregated, minority groups and others began to demand that American schools better reflect the diversity of its student body. There was an ever-growing cry for the inclusion of curricula that presented students with a variety of histories, models, and perspectives. During this time, the curricula that were developed were added to existing studies in an effort to provide something for everyone (this is what James Banks calls the "Additive Approach," which we discuss later in this chapter).

Banks uses the following definition of *multicultural education:* "a wide variety of programs and practices related to educational equity, women, ethnic groups, language minorities, low-income groups, and people with disabilities" (Banks & Banks, 2003, p. 6). To this definition, one might add "sexual orientation, religion, and learning styles." The phrase "related to," in Banks's definition leaves a great deal of room for interpretation. There are many different ways in which multicultural education gets enacted in the classroom.

On one level, multicultural education seeks to provide students with what Style (1988) refers to as "windows and mirrors" in the curriculum. In her monograph, Style refers to two Peanuts cartoons in which Snoopy ponders the old adage, "Beauty is only skin deep." He decides to change the adage to reflect his own identity and rewrites it as beauty is only "fur deep." In the next cartoon, Woodstock changes the phrase to read "feather deep."

Both Snoopy and Woodstock are interacting with this saying in a way that reflects their own individual identities—in other words, by looking into mirrors. However, Style proposes the need for balancing this tendency with windows through which to view cultures other than one's own. "Perhaps the truth that remains after such an exchange," she notes, "is simply that 'Beauty is'" (1988, n.p.).

An example of "windows" and "mirrors" can be found in the choice of literature students encounter in most American schools today. There exists what is called the "Western Canon," which contains certain "important" works of writing. Most students, for example, will read Edgar Allan Poe, Mark Twain, Emily Dickinson, or Shakespeare at some point in their school careers; students in more progressive programs also may encounter Toni Morrison, Gabriel García Márquez, Alice Walker, and other more contemporary authors. However, as Style points out, students should also be provided with windows through which to view cultures and peoples other than their own. To continue with our example, we might add other authors to the required reading lists such as Amy Tan, Leslie Marmon Silko, or Ralph Ellison. Adding diverse authors to a reading list is an example of Banks' (Banks & Banks, 2003) Additive Approach.

Banks, often referred to as the father of multicultural education, has theorized four different ways of implementing a multicultural curriculum—the Contributions Approach, the Additive Approach, the Transformation Approach, and the Social Action Approach. By viewing these approaches through the lens of Freire's *conscientização*—"learning to perceive social, political, and economic contradictions, and to take action against the oppressive elements of reality" (Ramos, translator's note in Freire [2003], p. 35), we see that they provide the educator with a continuum of practices, beginning with the least progressive (the Contributions Approach) to the most liberational (the Social Action Approach).

The Contributions Approach

Teachers might make reference to a culture's most popular heroes, holidays, foods, or costumes. This approach often involves special festivals, performances, or celebrations.

The Additive Approach

In this approach, literature, concepts, or themes might be added to the curriculum. The curriculum as such is not changed, only broadened to include more information.

The Transformation Approach

Here the structure of the curriculum is changed to allow students to view concepts (e.g., in history or literature) from a variety of viewpoints.

The Social Action Approach

While studying a topic, students are encouraged to give opinions, make decisions, and take action on a subject. Students take an active role in the curriculum.

Following are examples of each of these curricular approaches:

The Contributions Approach	The Additive Approach
To celebrate "El Cinco de Mayo," a teacher plays Mexican music in class as she teaches the students a few phrases in Spanish. She explains the holiday to students and has them label the town of Puebla and color in a map of Mexico.	To expand on a study of the treatment of Native Americans during the formation of the United States, the teacher asks students to read about the arrival of Spanish conquerors in Mexico and their treatment of the indigenous peoples.
The Transformation Approach	**The Social Action Approach**
In studying the history of the conquest of Mexico, the teacher provides students with primary sources from that period that outline the historical events from the perspective of the Spanish as well as the Mexica (known as the Aztecs by North American scholars).	Students are asked to read a brief history of the Tarahumara of northern Mexico, and about problems in maintaining their native language. Students confront the issue of heritage speakers of Spanish in the United States and brainstorm ways in which their language might be maintained. They might then devise a plan to work with Spanish speakers in the community.

However multicultural education works in your school setting, it is important to remember the teacher's role of power in the classroom. Multicultural education happens not just in the books we read, the lessons we teach, or the celebrations we organize, but also in the arrangement of desks in the classroom, the ways in which we address our students, and the tasks we ask them to perform. Every element of the school experience can be seen as part of a multicultural curriculum. As teachers, we can chose to include or exclude cultures in our teaching. While few teachers would consciously exclude a student, often the most subtle of gestures—the way in which we call on students or the lessons we include or omit in a given curriculum unit—have the power to validate or invalidate students' identities.

When multicultural education is connected to a methodology of equity, this educational idea can serve to include students who might otherwise be marginalized in the broader society. It also is meant to inform students who are members of mainstream society of the injustices that exist. Thus, the purpose of multicultural education is to make students—as well as the adults that work with them on a daily basis—aware of the power struggles that pervade society. A person who is aware of social power dynamics is better equipped to take action against perceived injustices. Thus, multicultural education should provide all participants with the tools necessary to observe, analyze, and effect change in society. Freire (2003) would call this "critical consciousness." For example, it is not enough to simply learn about prejudice; an active multicultural pedagogy would address ways to ameliorate the problem.

In keeping with Freire's pedagogy of critical consciousness and action, Banks's Social Action Approach, and the general philosophy of this book, Gorski sees three simple goals for multicultural education:

1. the transformation of self;
2. the transformation of schools and schooling; and
3. the transformation of society. (2003, p. 13)

The goal of this book is to enable you, the reader, to *do* multicultural education (through interaction with the narratives, conversations with colleagues about the "Questions to Consider," and the suggested projects and activities), rather than merely read about it.

NARRATIVE 2

Before You Read

As a teacher in the United States, you can be sure to experience multicultural education initiatives at one point or another in your career. Your school might sponsor a "Multicultural Night" in which students perform and parents share traditional cuisine. Perhaps your English department's reading list includes authors from diverse ethnic and cultural backgrounds. Or maybe you have changed your curriculum to reflect your students' home cultures. One way or another, most teachers have had some experience with teaching multiculturally or about multicultural topics.

Before you read "It's Multicultural Week!" think about your school's multicultural activities. Does your school have a multicultural curriculum already in place? List five events, activities, or curricular components that you feel might be termed "multicultural education." Try to label each activity as one of Banks' four practices: the Contributions Approach, the Additive Approach, the Transformation Approach, or the Social Action Approach.

"It's Multicultural Week!"

She looked forward to it every year. "It's multicultural week next week," she'd say with a smile. "I just love all the colorful costumes that the kids wear. They dance so nicely—and all the ethnic food that they bring! We always put on such a nice show."

Every year my friend's school has its multicultural week as a means of showcasing the diversity of the student body. Dances, songs, skits, and food festivals fill the five days in May that comprise the celebration. Parents are invited, as well as other community members. One year, a local news station even reported on the festivities. But something about the week has always bothered me, and I finally told my friend about my concerns.

"It's just one week, though. What about the rest of the year?" I asked.

My friend was confused. "We celebrate the students' cultures every day in many ways," she replied, somewhat defensively. "I always encourage my kids to say things in their language or to bring in their foods during snack time."

"Yes," I answered, "but what about the curriculum?"

"Well, come on, I mean, this is America. Shouldn't these kids learn what it means to be American?" Rather than ask my friend if she could adequately define what being American meant, I let it go and decided that it wasn't worth the effort. I had had this discussion before and didn't really want to rehash it.

My friend, like many veteran teachers of her generation, saw her own immigrant parents struggle with a new language and customs. They suppressed their heritage in order to be more "American." They refused to speak their native language to their children in an effort to expose them only to English. With this sort of background, it's no wonder that she is ambivalent to the idea of multicultural education. While my friend seems genuinely interested in her students' cultures and enjoys the yearly celebration in the gym, the theater, or the cafeteria, she is not so willing to change what happens inside the classroom. She's more than happy to add a few celebrations now and again, but the curriculum seems fine to her the way it is.

In my own teaching, I constantly look for ways to share with my students information about other cultures. I try to expose them to ideas and realities that might not have occurred to them before. One such lesson involved a simulation surrounding antigay prejudice and related derogatory comments.

As in most schools across the country, most negative comments, racial slurs, and other signs of prejudice are not accepted. Students listen to motivational speakers on topics such as bullying, harassment, or discrimination. They may see posters hung around the school that promote acceptance of diversity and difference. They may even join anti-bias clubs or participate in rallies or other demonstrations against racism, sexism, or even elitism. But the slurs that I hear most often in my middle school—and the ones that never seem to be caught by teachers or administrators and thus, continue to proliferate—are homophobic comments. It seems as if homophobia is the one remaining acceptable prejudice in today's schools.

After hearing "You fag!," "That's soooo gay," and "What a queer!," in the middle school hallways far too many times to count, I decided to act. My first attempt at halting these comments involved simply yelling at the offender. This student bowed his head, walked away, and surely continued to use these epithets, though no longer in my presence. For my second attempt, I stopped a student, pulled her aside into an empty room, and asked her to think about what she was saying. She said that she was "only kidding" and that the word "gay" was simply being used to describe something silly, foolish, or weird. This comment stunned me and made me rethink my plan of action. For the third attempt, I confided to the unwitting student that my best friend is gay and that I was personally hurt by his comments. This method seemed to reach deeper with the student than the other ones. However, a week after the student apologized to me and promised never to say such things again, I overheard him call another boy "a sissy freak." Back to the drawing board . . .

I felt as if I had to do something, however small, in an effort to make students understand why these comments were harmful. I decided on a two-day simulation that would get students more in touch with the challenges of being gay in our society. I asked them to think about topics of conversation that reveal whether they are straight or gay. They brainstormed a list of words like "girlfriends," "boyfriends," "dating," "crushes," and "hotties." They giggled as they made their list and with each term, boys and girls alike chatted eagerly at their tables about who likes who, what pop stars are "fine," and which students have already gone out on dates.

After collecting this list of topics, I gave students their assignment. They were to refrain for two days from talking about any topic that would reveal their sexual preference. This meant that students could not say "he's so cute!," "Justin really likes you," or "I think Brad Pitt is a hottie!" I asked them to write their feelings about the experiment in a journal at the end of both days. Since these types of conversations are ubiquitous in the middle school setting, the task was a challenging one. Students eagerly agreed to take part in the experiment, but soon found themselves unpleasantly surprised.

Later the first day, several students came to me and reported that the project was impossible. They could not stop talking about the banned topics and they were having a hard time watching what they felt to be their every word. I encouraged students to continue with the experiment and to do their best. The responses in their journals highlighted the frustration they were feeling: "EVERYthing I say is about boys," one girl wrote, adding, "What else IS there?"

After the two days had passed, we discussed the students' reactions to the project. They were amazed at how much their talk revealed their sexual preference. I then asked students to imagine a gay student in our school. The students gasped and giggled. "Do you think that a gay student feels comfortable talking about crushes in front of you?"—absolute silence. I continued, "When you are all talking about 'hotties' and 'cute boys,' can a student who is gay do the same?"

I meant the question to be rhetorical, but then one student raised his hand and said, "They can't. They have to lie, right? Like . . . ALL the time!" This student looked slightly pained at this realization.

Others nodded and looked down at their desks. "So, gay students have to sort of make believe and hide their true feelings. They have to be someone who they are not," one particularly sensitive girl added. "Wow . . ."

I ended the lesson by expressing my sadness at the negative and harmful comments that I often hear in the hallways and cafeteria against homosexuals. I told the students that, along with having to hide their identity and live a lie, gay students, teachers, and others have to hear mean comments said about them every day—sometimes coming from their own friends. I asked students to stop using these slurs and to stand strong when they heard others using them. The bell rang and my kids poured into the hallway, where we could all hear "you faggot!" loud and clear as the periods changed and students ran to their next class.

I am not naïve enough to think that this simulation activity will eradicate the antigay sentiment in my school, nor will it stop the thoughtless name-calling in the hallways and in the cafeteria. I do think, however, that my students, at least, may think twice before using the terms. It has at least sensitized them to some of the realities of being a closeted gay person in our school and made them aware of how transparently they reveal their own identities to others.

My friend's multicultural celebration is a decidedly more fun activity than my simulation lesson. It surely gets more praise from parents, as well. However, if I have changed even one student's attitude and curtailed even a few derogatory comments in my school, I feel as if having fun can wait.

Questions to Consider

1. Using Banks's terminology, what approach would you say best describes the narrator's lesson? How would you describe the narrator's friend's multicultural celebration?

2. Why do you think the narrator's friend looks forward to multicultural week so much? What do you think her opinion would be of the narrator's lesson? Why do you think this?

3. Why do you think the narrator chose not to confront her friend about their difference of opinion? Can you think of a time when you decided to suppress your feelings on a similar topic with a colleague? How might the narrator have confronted her friend in a constructive way?

4. In what ways does the narrator's lesson help students to understand the social difficulties faced by closeted gay students? What, if anything, does the narrator do with her students to avoid stereotypical views of homosexuals?

5. What are the differences between role play and simulation? What are some benefits and drawbacks of each for teaching multiculturally?

6. In the last paragraph, the narrator alludes to the reaction of parents to both her and her friend's lessons. How would parents react to the narrator's lesson in your school? Would you be able to carry out such an activity in your classroom? Why or why not? What, if anything, would parents object to?

NARRATIVE 3

Before You Read

Multicultural education does not involve only the lessons we teach, the books we read, or the celebrations we organize. Interactions between teachers and students convey messages of expectations, order, and acceptance. Rules in the broader society and cultural stereotypes, both positive and negative, are often perpetuated in schools.

Think about the different cultural groups that exist in your school. Are there stereotypes (positive or negative) about a particular group with regard to school performance? Do students of a particular group have an image of being "smart," "weak," "good athletes," or "artistic"? Think about some of your own students and the expectations that you or your colleagues may project onto them. Do these expectations affect the choices that you make about those students? About the curriculum you teach? About how you communicate with them in class? If so, in what ways?

Beyond the Label

Two decades ago, a rural central New Jersey community burgeoned with development. Corporate America discovered low tax rates and the opportunity for expansion in an area on the major Northeastern corridor that bisects the state. Our very small school district with a reputation for excellence attracted educationally minded families from, literally, all over the world. Within a decade, the district quadrupled in size, with an increase in student diversity. By the mid 1990s, 82 different languages and dialects were counted in the district. The current demographics of the 1,100 students in the middle school in this story are 62 percent white, 29 percent Asian, 4 percent Hispanic, and 5 percent African American.

Three of my favorite students, Priya, Mimi, and Laura, are all classified as "Asian" in the reports to the state. They are eighth graders in our middle school who were designated as "gifted and talented" in school records. Laura and Mimi qualify for the elite "accelerated and enriched" math class. Mimi opted out.

One day, these three girls were chuckling over a sheet that Mimi had printed out from the Internet called, "How to Be the Perfect Asian Kid." Included on the list were such terms as "smart," "good in math," "plays violin and piano," and "well-behaved." From their comments, it was apparent that they are aware of the fact that they are labeled as "Asian" and "smart." They then recalled specific teacher comments made on report cards or progress reports that reinforce these labels. The following anecdotes are taken directly from reflections the girls wrote regarding their experiences with being stuck in the stereotype.

"Priya's performance in math class does not live up to expectations." Priya replies, "Whose expectations?"

"I was born in New Jersey, though I am of pure Indian descent, and I do consider myself an Indian rather than an American. At first glance, I'm your stereotypical Asian American girl. I get good grades, I play the piano and violin, and I have a reputation for academic excellence among both my teachers and peers. Though I have an incredibly defiant and opinioned personality, in school I wear a benign, obedient façade, since I've found both teachers and students react much more comfortably when I feign passivity. It happens that one of my weakest areas in school is math—I grant you, a fairly rare situation for an Asian. I get decent grades in math (report card grades in all subjects, including math, are As.) but it has been substantially more difficult for me than other subjects. This year, when midterm reports for the first quarter were sent home, I was scraping by with a 92 percent average—my only A–. In the comment section the teacher wrote, 'Results from Chapters 1 and 2 were less than expected.'

"Now, considering that this was the very first unit of the school year, and this comment came from a teacher who was new to the school and had no knowledge of me, her 'expectations,' I assume, are based on prejudices—I am Indian, and do well in all my other classes, therefore I must be slacking off in math. I've found this is one of the most difficult parts of being a 'gifted' Indian student. Excellence is expected every time for everything: an A– just isn't considered enough. In a situation where I am less than talented, both teachers and students remind me continually that I have not reached the potential that they have somehow predetermined that I have. What presumptuous teachers have yet to realize is that assumed intelligence can often be more of a hassle than an asset for a student."

"Mimi is an excellent student." Mimi replies, "With an attitude!"

'Now, what have you noticed about how Asian women usually act towards men?' my social studies teacher asks during our unit on China.

One of my American friends raises her hand and says, 'Well, they are usually meek, quiet and they defer to men.'

'Excuse me!' I yelp, as I turn in my seat to face her. 'Meek? Quiet? Deferential to men? What are you talking about?'

"Then I realize she is just repeating the common stereotype of Asians—and not just of Asian women. According to these presumptions, we Asians are supposed to be a bunch of conservative, eyeglass-wearing nerdy kids who are afraid of confrontation. We're the ones who put our heads down and do all the work, never uttering a word of complaint. In our school with almost a third Asian kids, we have our share of this type of student. However, I do not count myself in their number. While I wear glasses, keep a straight A average in all of my classes, and work hard at school, I am far from meek and quiet. I break from the stereotype, a good little Asian girl who is not afraid to voice her opinions. At the beginning of the school year, when my teachers first experienced my attitude, they were obviously taken aback.

'Whoa, where did that come from?'

"Here was a Chinese girl, hanging with other Asians, smart and all—but me, not so silent. After a while, however, they adjusted to the fact that I am opinionated and not shy about voicing my thoughts. I do not believe that the old stereotypes can be applied to this generation of Asians, for we are no longer just good at math. Many have traded their glasses for contacts and many are far from conservative. No longer are we the old Asians, but the AzN generation—proud of where we came from and possessing a serious attitude. AzN PrYdE."

"Laura should speak out more." Laura replies, "Look at what I do, not what I say."

"Like Priya and Mimi, I can say I am 100 percent, in this case, Japanese. I am also fifth generation Japanese-American (gosei). I do fit the stereotype that hassles Priya. I am good in math. I really like math. And unlike Mimi, I am the quiet, very quiet, Asian kid. However, I do not play violin or piano. I don't play any musical instrument. What I do play is sports, in particular, soccer. In this, I am outside the stereotype, a fact of which I have often been reminded.

"Since second grade I have been playing soccer. I joined a travel soccer team in fourth grade, then advanced to 'play up' with girls a year or two older than me. At the beginning of my eighth-grade year, I decided to join, for the first time, a school soccer team. The coach, who was also one of my teachers, had never seen me play and had not heard about me. The two best players on the school team are on my travel team where I am their starting center half, which is the equivalent of a quarterback in football. But somehow for half of our school season, I was the substitute and only allowed to play for about five minutes. My coach had no reason to bench me. I never missed a practice, never gave him any attitude (I'm the quiet one, remember?), and the only people he could have consulted about my skills, if he were so inclined, were my travel soccer friends, who would have acknowledged me as their equal.

"The rest of the team also wondered why I was a substitute, and even the girl who played my position wanted me to start. However, I would not make an issue about playing because this was my teacher and I could not disrespect him. Long after the season ended, I would have to live with what he thought of me. The only reason I can think of for my being benched is that my coach assumed I was inept. I gave him no reason to think this, and my short field performances were fine. Perhaps it was because I am Japanese American. Asians, after all, don't do sports."

What Priya, Mimi, and Laura reveal is that they are proud of their heritage, but also proud of their individuality. Though they celebrate their ethnicity, they resent when "Asian" and "smart" are used as labels to define who they are. What they also reveal in their commentaries is that they are middle schoolers—respectful, yet wary of teachers' attitudes, and conscious of what their peers think. A starting point to connect with students is to first know and support them by their age. Middle school students, regardless of ethnicity and socioeconomic status, share recognizable developmental patterns, physically, cognitively, and psychologically. What each of these young women is saying is "Look at who I am, look at what I can do." They are "Asian," "smart," and so much more.

Questions to Consider

1. The author writes about labels commonly attributed to Asians. Have you heard these labels before? Do you know students to whom they apply? Do you know students who break the stereotypes?
2. Priya shows internalization of one of the stereotypes she criticizes when she says, "It happens that one of my weakest areas in school is math—I grant you, a fairly rare situation for an Asian." Do any of the girls show this internalization elsewhere?
3. What are some of the stereotypes for your own ethnic/cultural group? Are they valid? If so, in what ways? If not, why not?
4. Have you ever told a student that she is "not working up to expectations?" Do you expect the same level of work from all of your students?
5. Mimi uses the spelling *AzN PrYdE* ("Asian Pride") to express her identity. Have you seen any other new spellings of words or new terms that students

have created to describe themselves? Why do you think they choose to write in this way?

6. What stereotypes have you encountered relating to students who play sports? Those who play musical instruments? Those who get good grades? Do you have students who fit into these categories? How do other students/faculty treat them?

Project and Extension Activities

1. Look at the cartoon at the start of this chapter. Which of Banks's four approaches best describes the practice of celebrating Black History Month and Women's History Month? Have you ever heard someone say, "What a shame that we have to have a Black (Women's) History Month at all! We should celebrate Black (Women's) history all the time!"? With a partner, create a short skit debating the values of Black and Women's History months. In your role play, include suggestions for ways in which black history and women's history might be "celebrated all the time."

2. Create a self-description:
   a. Step 1: Imagine that you are going to begin corresponding via email with a new "key pal." In a brief email, describe yourself to this new friend.
   b. Step 2: What characteristics did you choose to include in your email (gender, ethnicity, race, age, etc.)? Make a list. Observe which elements of your identity are most salient for you.
   c. Step 3: Write a list of descriptors for yourself using the following labels:
      • Race
      • Ethnicity
      • Socioeconomic status
      • Age
      • Religion
      • Gender
      • Sexual orientation
      • Family of origin
      • Region
      • Language
   d. Step 4: How did you feel as you were writing the first narrative description of yourself? How did you feel as you were writing the second, more succinct definition? Which description did you prefer writing? Why did you prefer one or the other?

3. Design a social action project. If you are currently teaching, think about your discipline, age group, and current curriculum. Design your project so that you can use it with your students. If you are not teaching, design a project that might be appropriate for use with a youth community group or in

another educational setting. Write a short lesson plan for the project (include rationale, goal, materials, and briefly detailed steps to carry out the lesson). Share your project with your colleagues.
4. Read this poem about a young girl's experience as a recent immigrant to the United States:

Chink

I remember that day,
my first day of school in America.
My mother dressed me in yellow,
my favorite color—yellow
shirt with little white ruffles clinging playfully to my collar,
yellow socks stretching for the sky,
yellow shorts (its front pleats crinkled like the folds of an oriental fan),
and a yellow Snoopy bag stuffed with
Pochacco pencils,
Crayola crayons,
and three green dollars for lunch.

I trustingly followed my parents and their dreams
into a country
of which I knew nothing,
but that its inhabitants had sparkling
ocean-blue eyes and golden hair that curled,
its newly elected president—a fallen
Hollywood star.

Hopeful of, no . . .
Obsessed with becoming the first immigrant
to master the English language in
one month
I would instead discover that within that month
I had mastered,
"My name is Seung Eun Lee."
As frustrated tears plunged from my chin into
the fan-folds of my yellow shorts, teachers
would ask with worried expressions,
"What's the matter? What's the matter?" and I would
reply with only a silent thought . . .
"Does it look like I need WATERMELONS?"

My mother was so proud when
I won the third grade Spelling Bee. I remember
seeing her pale face pop with exclamatory smiles

and her frail body perk-up in elation as I spelled
restaurant. R-e-s-t-a-u-r-a-n-t. Restaurant.
Had it been on the list, I would have also known how to spell
chink.
C-h-i-n-k.
Chink.

Although I was only eight,
I knew. Every morning I would wake up,
not to my mother's gentle kisses on my forehead,
but to my dad's droning engine sadly crying its
good-bye, as both left for work.
I would run after the car as it drove away
still squinty-eyed,
  puffy-faced,
        barefoot,
waving my bony hands in the crisp chill morning air.
Dad would brake—his expression
desperately expressionless, and I would
press my face up against the window panting my
good-byes and I'll-miss-yous
stretching my dry lips into an illuminating smile to reassure them that
"I'm a big girl now."
My mother's eyes would struggle not to
blink.
Mustering all her spirit, she would force a
smile and lovingly scold me for running out without my slippers, while
every "Good-bye," I yelped
every "I'll miss you," I whimpered
choked at her sense of purpose in landing on this country.

I stood in the middle of the street just
watching. Watching until the car became a mere silvery blur.
Watching the back of her head tilt forward with subtle jerks as
she sobbed.
I knew.

"I have half a heart."
That is what I told all my fourth grade pals
who mistook my identity for
an egg roll.
Weighing less than eighty pounds,
lacking physical prowess, and not yet having

perfected my command of English and particularly of
profanities (that made grammatical sense) in order to fight back,
lying about "half a heart" was my only defense . . . oh, and
"My brother has half a lung."

I remember
evesdropping on my mothers morning prayers and
straining my ears to make sure I heard my name,
feeling the hunger pang against my stomach as the scent of
her kimchee chigeh
s e e p e d into my room,
listening to the music of her spoons clanging against the pans,
her knives chop chop chopping away
in harmony with the boil boiling stew . . .
and her feet
shuffling
to these melodious tunes.
I long to be home again.

That first day of school in America,
my mother walked me to the
bus stop
to capture that pivotal moment on film.
The bus arrived in minutes.
What I felt the moment I released myself from her protective grip
I do not recall . . . the daunting task of connecting to this other world
by way of a shake or a nod lay ahead for the day.
I slowly walked up to the threshold of Americanization and upon
crossing over it
turned around, smiled courageously for the camera.
Chk. Chk.
The long yellow school bus and
my yellow ensemble filled the photograph.
I wonder
if one had to look hard to find me—the dark face of a little
Korean girl (with half a heart)
suspended in a big yellow glob.

How does the author feel about having come to America? How does language play a role in her interactions in school? Why do you think she describes herself as having "half a heart?" Write a poem about an immigration experience. It can be based on your own personal experiences, or those of a family member, colleague, or friend. Share your poem with your class.

5. Read this proclamation:

WHEREAS	our society is made up of many backgrounds and cultures, and
WHEREAS	we have many holidays which celebrate the customs and traditions of individual groups, but do not have a holiday which honors our great diversity of cultures, and
WHEREAS	the Village of Ridgewood has and continues to experience considerable diversification in the cultural and racial composition of its population, and
WHEREAS	the future strength of our society depends upon people of good will continuing to work for the elimination of racial and cultural prejudice in our society, and
WHEREAS	there is strength in diversity when each individual understands and appreciates his or her own uniqueness and has a sincere appreciation for the cultures of others, and
WHEREAS	the Ridgewood Board of Education recognizes the recommendation of the CONVO '92 students, and its own continued commitment to increase awareness and appreciation of diverse cultures.
NOW THEREFORE	be it resolved that the Ridgewood Board of Education proclaim the Friday before the official observance of Columbus Day, CULTURAL ALLADAY, an annual recognition of the cultural diversity within our own community and society at large.

What label would Banks use to describe this approach to multicultural education? What types of activities might occur on "Cultural Alladay?" What would a proclamation look like for your school context? Write one for your school/district/community. Submit it to your school administration, Board of Education, or local Council or Assembly representative.

6. Title VIII of the Civil Rights Act of 1968 (Fair Housing Act), prohibits the discrimination in the sale, rental, and financing of dwellings, and in other housing-related transactions, based on race, color, national origin, religion, sex, familial status, and handicap (disability). Look at the following policy guidelines from the HUD (U.S. Department of Housing and Urban Development) website (Achtenberg, 1995, n.p.) regarding appropriate and inappropriate wording of housing advertisements (emphasis in original):

a. Race, color, national origin. Real estate advertisements should state no discriminatory preference or limitation on account of race, color, or national origin. Use of words describing the housing, the current or potential residents, or the neighbors or neighborhood in racial or ethnic terms (i.e., **white family home, no Irish**) will create liability under this section.

b. **Religion.** Advertisements should not contain an explicit preference, limitation or discrimination on account of religion (i.e., **no Jews, Christian home**). Advertisements which use the legal name of an entity which contains a religious reference (for example, **Roselawn Catholic Home),** or those which contain a religious symbol, (such as **a cross),** standing alone, may indicate a religious preference. . . .

c. **Sex.** Advertisements for single-family dwellings or separate units in a multi-family dwelling should contain no explicit preference, limitation or discrimination based on sex.

d. **Handicap.** Real estate advertisements should not contain explicit exclusions, limitations, or other indications of discrimination based on handicap (i.e., **no wheelchairs).**

e. **Familial status.** Advertisements may not state an explicit preference, limitation or discrimination based on familial status. Advertisements may not contain limitations on the number or ages of children, or state a preference for adults, couples or singles.

Look through the real estate section of your local newspaper, paying close attention to the housing advertisements. Do any ads violate the Fair Housing Act? Imagine that you are going to rent or sell your home. Write an advertisement that would be acceptable under the Act.

7. Read these quotes referring to the United States as a "melting pot" (Thinkexist .com, 2005; Bartleby.com, 2005):

> America is God's Crucible, the great Melting-Pot where all the races of Europe are melting and re-forming!
>
> **Israel Zangwill, 1864–1926**
> **English Writer**

> We become not a melting pot but a beautiful mosaic. Different people, different beliefs, different yearnings, different hopes, different dreams.
>
> **Jimmy Carter, 1924–**
> **39th U.S. President**

> The metaphor of the melting pot is unfortunate and misleading. A more accurate analogy would be a salad bowl, for, though the salad is an entity, the lettuce can still be distinguished from the chicory, the tomatoes from the cabbage.
>
> **Carl N. Degler, 1921–**
> **Historian**

Do you agree with the use of the term *melting pot?* Why or why not? How do you feel about the term *beautiful mosaic?* Create a new phrase that you feel best describes the United States in terms of its multicultural identity.

Cultural Exploration

1. *Explore other schools:* Do a search on the Web for school sites that describe their multicultural curricula or activities. Find a description that corresponds to each of Banks's four practices (the Contributions, Additive, Transformation, and Social Action approaches). For each of the descriptions that you find for the Contributions, Additive, and Transformation approaches, brainstorm ways in which a Social Action Approach component might be built into each activity.

   For example:

Contributions Approach	Additive Approach	Transformation Approach	Social Action Approach
An elementary school in California provides a link on their Web page that lists "Winter holidays around the world," including the Hmong New Year.	Add *Dia's Story Cloth* and study Hmong quilts to a unit on stories about immigration.	View the video *Being Hmong Means Being Free.* Compare the experiences of the Hmong and the Vietcong during the Vietnam War.	Establish a cooperative in which Hmong story quilts can be sold, with proceeds going to the creation of educational materials.

2. *Explore the Web:* The Internet is full of information about diversity and multiculturalism. Find the following:
   - Three websites devoted to "hate" messages (these might be personal webpages, the homepage of the KKK, etc.)
   - Three websites devoted to tolerance aimed at adults
   - Three websites devoted to multicultural education aimed at children or young adults

   Write a review of the websites that includes the following information:
   - The name of the website
   - The address (begin with "http://")
   - Who is/are the author(s) or sponsor(s)? (Is the author/sponsor obviously posted on the page?)
   - Who is the site's primary intended audience? What is its intended goal? Is it stated explicitly on the site?
   - Description of the site (graphics? textual content? interactivity? number of pages?)
   - Would you recommend this website to children? To young adults? To adults?

3. *Explore teaching materials:* Textbooks are laden with cultural references. In your school or local library, find four textbooks in your field. Analyze the cultural references in the texts. Answer the following questions about each text:
   - What is the title/subject of the text?
   - Who are the authors?
   - When and where was the text published?
   - How can you classify the majority of the cultural references in the texts? (e.g., "White males?" "Western writers?")
   - Can you identify any stereotypes that the authors have internalized? If so, which ones?
   - What assumptions can you identify that the text's authors are making about their audience?

   Do a quantitative analysis of the different cultural groups represented in the text. Create some sort of visual representation of the data (bar graph, pie chart, etc).

 Internet Connection

The National Association for Multicultural Education (NAME)

Offers visitors to the site access to a vast store of information on issues surrounding multicultural education in the United States. You can read and download position papers adopted by NAME on such topics as Affirmative Action and Social Justice. Contains information about local NAME chapters and conferences and institutes offered across the country. There is also a link to resources such as available grants, journals, and research.
http://www.nameorg.org

Tolerance.org

Sponsored by the Southern Poverty Law Center, this multifaceted site provides teachers, parents, teens, and kids resources and activities for exploring diversity issues. For teachers, the site provides resources, development tools, and grant information, as well as online lessons and activities for the classroom. Also on the site is information about how to order a variety of free teacher materials such as *Teaching Tolerance* magazine, videos, and posters for your school.
http://www.tolerance.org

The Diversity Database

Created and maintained by the University of Maryland, this database provides links to multicultural and diversity resources. Included in the site are definitions,

directories, syllabi, and statistical information on a variety of topics. You can connect to specific information from other colleges and universities about their diversity programs. Click on the "Diversity" tab at the bottom of the page, then on "Web Resources," then on "Diversity Database" [or go directly to *http://www.inform.umd.edu/EdRes/Topic/Diversity*].
http://www.umd.edu

The Multicultural Pavilion

This comprehensive website offers visitors links to research, downloadable fact sheets, and social justice speeches as well as opportunities to submit articles, share creative writing, or join the listserv.
http://www.edchange.org

References and Recommended Reading

Achtenberg, R. (1995). *Guidance regarding advertisements under §804(c) of the Fair Housing Act.* Memorandum. Washington, DC: U.S. Department of Housing and Urban Development. Retrieved 24 May 2005 from www.hud.gov/offices/fheo/disabilities/sect804achtenberg.pdf

Banks, J. A. (2002). *An introduction to multicultural education,* 3rd ed. Boston: Allyn & Bacon.

Banks, J. A., & Banks, C. A. (2003). *Multicultural education: Issues and perspectives.* New York: John Wiley & Sons.

Bartleby.com. (2005). Quotations. Retrieved from http://www.bartleby.com/73/49.html

Bigelow, B., Christensen, L., Karp, S., Miner, B. & Peterson, B. (Eds.). (1994). *Rethinking our classrooms: Teaching for equity and justice.* Montgomery, AL: Rethinking Schools, Ltd.

Brown, S. C., & Kysilka, M. L. (2002). *Applying multicultural and global concepts in the classroom and beyond.* Boston: Allyn & Bacon.

Davidman, L., & Davidman, P. (1997). *Teaching with a multicultural perspective: A practical guide.* White Plains, NY: Longman.

Dresser, N. (1996). *Multicultural manners: New rules of etiquette for a changing society.* Hoboken, NJ: Wiley.

Freire, P. (2003). *Pedagogy of the oppressed.* New York: Continuum.

Gorski, P. (2003). *Multicultural education and the Internet: Intersections and integrations,* 2nd ed. New York: McGraw-Hill.

Grant, C. A., & Lei, J. (2001). *Global constructions of multicultural education: Theories and realities.* Mahwah, NJ: Lawrence Erlbaum Associates.

Grant, C. A., & Sleeter, C. E. (2003). *Turning on learning: Five approaches for multicultural teaching plans for race, class, gender and disability.* New York: John Wiley & Sons.

Hollins, E. (1996). *Culture in school learning: Revealing the deep meaning.* Mahwah, NJ: Lawrence Erlbaum Associates.

Lee, E., Menkart, D., & Okazawa-Rey, M. (Eds.). (1998). *Beyond heroes and holidays: A practical guide to K–12 anti-racist, multicultural education and staff development.* Washington, DC: Teaching for Change.

Lisi, P., & Rios, F. (Eds.). (2005). *Multicultural perspectives: The official journal of the National Association for Multicultural Education.* Vol. 7. Mahwah, NJ: Lawrence Erlbaum Associates.

Moya, P. M. L. (2002). *Learning from experience: Minority identities, multicultural struggles.* Berkeley/Los Angeles: University of California Press.

Nieto, S. (1999). *The light in their eyes: Creating multicultural learning communities.* New York: Teachers College Press.

Reissman, R. (1994). *The evolving multicultural classroom.* Alexandria, VA: Association for Supervision and Curriculum Development.

Shulman, J., & Mesa-Bains, A. (1993). *Diversity in the classroom: A casebook for teachers and teacher educators.* Mahwah, NJ: Lawrence Erlbaum Associates.

Sleeter, C. E., & Grant, C. A. (2003). *Making choices for multicultural education: Five approaches to race, class, and gender.* New York: John Wiley & Sons.

Style, E. (1988). Curriculum as window and mirror. In *Listening for all voices* (n.p). Monograph. Summit, NJ: Oak Knoll School. Retrieved from http://www.enc.org/topics/equity/articles/document.shtm?input=ACQ-111548-1548

Takaki, R. (1993). *A different mirror: A history of multicultural America.* New York: Little, Brown.

ThinkExist.com. (2005). Quotations. Retrieved from http:// en.thinkexist.com/search/searchquotation.asp?search=melting+pot

Tiedt, P. L., & Tiedt, I. M. (2002). *Multicultural teaching: A handbook of activities, information, and resources.* Boston: Allyn & Bacon.

Race and
Ethnicity

A Place to Begin

Educational researcher and theorist Michael Apple has written extensively on the topic of curriculum and issues of power in education. He examines Spencer's original question, "What knowledge is of most worth?" (Spencer, 1889, as cited in Apple, 1990, p. 47), and encourages teachers to think of teaching as an eminently political act. We often think that we enter the classroom devoid of an agenda aside from the goal of educating our students in math, science, physical education—whatever our speciality might be. Apple asserts that the curriculum we teach (content) and how we teach it (form) are both political acts with specific political results.

Consider this example: In teaching a unit about the family, we might be tempted to ask students to trace their family history back as far as they can and to create a family tree with the information. Aside from the logistical difficulties that kids from "nontraditional" families have with this assignment (stepfamilies, adopted children, half siblings, etc.), African American students will also find this project to be challenging at best. Consider the history of African Americans in this country (or, more generally, of people of African descent throughout the Americas). When Africans were taken to the Americas to work as slaves, they were torn from their families and forced to begin life anew divorced from their relatives. An African American child who can trace her family back to slave times is prone to construct a family tree with few roots. Thus, a simple activity—the ubiquitous family tree assignment—brings up political and social issues for a segment of the classroom population.

Hegemony

Like Freire, Apple (1990) highlights the connections between entrenched school structures and the perpetuation of the status quo. As active participants in schools, teachers play an important role in supporting these connections. He states, "The educational institutions are usually the main agencies of transmission of an effective dominant culture" (p. 6). He describes curricula as being overt and hidden. The *overt curriculum* in your school includes the scope and sequence of your textbook, the curriculum documents for your subject area, and the standards put forth by your professional organization for a given grade and topic. Examples of the *hidden curriculum* include the topics that are excluded from your scope and sequence and the ways in which students are encouraged (or not encouraged) to participate in class discussions and activities.

Let's look again at our family tree project example. Examining the hidden curriculum of such a project reveals the assumption that a "normal" family is one that can be traced back for many generations and one that fits neatly into the linear format of the branches of the tree image. A student who encounters such an assignment generally assumes, because of the teacher's status as an authority figure, that it is both appropriate and feasible. If this student cannot complete the task, or has difficulty doing so, he naturally tends to believe that it is through some fault of his own, not that the task is inherently flawed. Such hidden messages, all transmitted with little or no conscious attention on the part of the teacher or student, are powerful, and serve to maintain the status quo and power balance in the teacher–student relationship.

The hegemonic forces at play in schools dictate certain rules and norms that may or may not be obvious to an observer, or even to the participants themselves. To look at another example, consider the unspoken rule that students should not call out when the teacher is talking. On the surface, this rule seems perfectly reasonable, since if students kept interrupting, the teacher might not be able to complete a lesson within the allowed time. Furthermore, we see this rule as enforcing proper respect for elders and decorum in general in the classroom. However, it also serves to maintain the power balance in the classroom, with the teacher being in charge and the student being subservient. Freire's idea of a praxis in which teacher and student converse freely in an even exchange about a problem of importance to both parties does not seem to fit with the structure of today's American classroom. Both Freire and Apple would view the American educational system as perpetuating the agenda of the majority over the needs of the minority.

Constructing the "Other"

Given recent concerns over illiteracy, falling test scores, and student failures—especially in schools with a predominantly minority student body—accountability has become more and more an issue on many Americans' minds. Apple (1990) proposes the idea that the focus has shifted from attention to meeting the educational needs of traditionally disadvantaged groups such as African Americans, English Language Learners, and students in inner-city schools to providing these groups with "free choice" to move from one school to another in search of an adequate education.

This push toward a "free market economy" in school, exemplified by school choice and the voucher system, reveals an attempt to change public schooling by forcing schools to compete for "clients." The aim is ostensibly to allow students the ability to go where the educational programs will best suit their needs, but the side effect of such a program is the construction of the identity of the "other." A meritocracy results in which, rather than repairing failing schools, students are given the option of changing to a "better" educational setting. Students who are not able to find their way to a better school, for any number of reasons—economic (i.e., parents cannot afford to get their children to the new school), cultural (i.e., parents do not want their students traveling too far away from home), or linguistic (i.e., parents are not fully aware of the opportunities available due to language and/or cultural barriers)—are *left behind* in a school that is uncared for and inferior. Since those students who are brighter or simply more mobile flee the struggling school, the mix of students in that school becomes less and less heterogeneous. The "better" schools keep getting better and the struggling schools continue to struggle.

The No Child Left Behind Act of 2001 (NCLB) is another extension of this attention to accountability. In an effort to establish the same academic standards for all students, the NCLB legislation requires school districts to "raise the bar" without giving much thought to the ways in which certain groups of students in the United States have been marginalized in the school system. It raises the bar without examining the nature of the hurdle.

Labels also play an important role in constructing the "other." Racial and ethnic epithets are often used as a means of distancing one group from another (i.e., when a member of a majority group uses a racial epithet with a member of a minority group.) However, racial and ethnic terms are often reappropriated by members of a group to assert control over the words that had served to oppress them. For example, the term *nigger,* is racist and offensive when used by a white person towards a black person. However, blacks often use the term with each other as a means of neutralizing its meaning and taking ownership of it.

Labels, however, are not always so overtly controversial. Take, for example, the terms *Latino* versus *Hispanic*. *Hispanic* refers to people who can trace their ancestry to Spain or Latin America. *Latino,* on the other hand, refers more to language of origin, being a term describing any native speaker of a Latin-based language. It thus is a broader term, including those with African, Asian, and Native American identities. Some object to the term *Hispanic,* since many feel that it was invented specifically with the United States census in mind, as a means of classifying Spanish speakers without a full understanding of the range of Latin American racial and ethnic identities. How would a Guatemalan-born Spanish speaker of African descent living in the United States define herself, for example? African American, Latin American, Hispanic—or all three?

Often we may hear our colleagues say, "I don't see color. All of my kids are the same." While we may see this philosophy as treating all students equally, despite race or ethnicity, we are actually doing kids a disservice by ignoring their cultures and individual realities. It is crucial that we see the differences. Simply seeing, however, is not enough. We must also acknowledge diversity and work towards equitable educational experiences and opportunities for all.

NARRATIVE 4

Before You Read

How do you define yourself in racial and/or ethnic terms? Are you comfortable with your racial and ethnic identity? Why or why not?

Think about your school. Are you part of the racial or ethnic majority? The minority? What are the advantages or disadvantages to your status? Is there a racial or ethnic minority community in your school? If so, are there any inequalities that you can identify with regard to this/these group(s)? Compare your racial/ethnic status to that of your students.

Silly Chinese Girl

My first substitute teaching experience was for Ms. Sobel's second-grade class at a public school. The classroom consisted of about 70 percent Caucasian children and 30 percent minorities, which included Latin Americans, Chinese Americans, and one African American boy. I considered this group of children to be extremely diverse in comparison to my own elementary school experience at the same school over a decade earlier.

I learned a great deal that day from Ms. Sobel's notes and lesson plan, and from just being with the students in the classroom. For the most part, the children seemed bright and very well behaved. However, there was one Chinese boy named Terrence who gave me a hard time. Terrence talked in the middle of a lesson and distracted other children. He played during story time and refused to do some of his assignments. Ms. Sobel had warned me that Terrence and two or three other children might be talkative or overly energetic, but I was not prepared for the way Terrence defied me at times.

"He seemed fine when Ms. Sobel was still in the room," I thought to myself. "Maybe it's the fact that I'm a sub and kids know they can take advantage of the situation." So I just dismissed his behavior.

A week later I was called back to sub at the school again. I was happy to return and was now in Ms. Alan's first-grade classroom. When my kids had an assembly, I was called to briefly watch Ms. Sobel's group while she conducted some tests for at-risk readers in the hallway. I was glad to return to this class since I had already learned all the children's names and had enjoyed the group the previous week.

I started to read them a book. The children sat very quietly and were all quite attentive, except for Terrence, who wriggled in his seat. Both Ms. Arthur, a volunteer from a local college, and I had to ask Terrence several times to stop distracting others. He sat still for a while, but in the middle of the story, Terrence mumbled under his breath rather loudly, "You silly Chinese girl!"

I heard exactly what he said, but I asked him to repeat it. He refused. I said, "Terrence if you have something to share, please say it aloud".

He shook his head with an expression of neither fear nor regret. I felt like he was testing me! Hurt, I could feel the warmth of embarrassment and shock rise to the back of my neck. I couldn't for the life of me know what to say. All the children stared at me waiting for a reaction, and I could feel Ms. Arthur' eyes watching me. Those two or three seconds felt like an eternity to me. I just wanted to crawl into a hole and die. But instead, I said, "Terrence, I heard what you said. That was very disrespectful of you. My name is Ms. Ma, not, 'silly Chinese girl'. Do you understand? You are never to say that again or I will go to the office and call your mother and you can tell her what you said to the teacher. I will speak to Ms. Sobel about this."

I could hear my voice breaking up over some of the words. I could feel my hand shaking as I spoke. I wasn't angry, not really, just terribly embarrassed and hurt for some reason. I could not understand why I felt so hurt. As I finished, Terrence just sat there staring at me blankly. I didn't care. I tried to pretend as if nothing happened and went back to reading the story with a great big smile. The children clapped at the end of the story and then wrote in their journals. Twenty minutes later, Ms. Sobel returned and I mentioned the incident to her. She immediately apologized and told me she would speak to his mother. I thanked her and went back to my first graders upstairs. I taught Ms. Alan's class math and writing and didn't give Terrence or what he had said a second thought, believing, or maybe wanting to believe, that it was of no consequence to me that this kid was rude.

At the end of the day I ran into Ms. Sobel as I was clocking out. She told me she had spoken with Mrs. Tan, Terrence's mom, and that she had not seemed the least bit surprised. Mrs. Tan explained to Ms. Sobel that Terrence had been going through a self-hate phase. He refused to speak Chinese at home like he used to. He refused to eat Chinese food or to acknowledge that he was Chinese! He would say, "I'm American, not stupid Chinese."

His parents both talked to him about his attitude with no results. Mrs. Tan told Ms. Sobel that Terrence has been feeling ashamed of his culture and sees it as inferior to American culture, and asked Ms. Sobel to extend her apologies to me. I thanked Ms. Sobel and told her that I understood, explaining that I too, had experienced a similar self-hating phase like Terrence was experiencing now.

Later that night, I could not stop thinking about what had happened. I felt that I had given the wrong response to Terrence in that classroom. I should have proudly acknowledged that I am Chinese and said that he must be proud too, but that in the classroom he would have to address me as Ms. Ma or teacher and nothing else. I should have asked to speak with Mrs. Tan myself and taken Terrence aside to speak to him privately about the matter instead of just addressing him in the classroom. I should not have said, "I will speak to Ms. Sobel about your behavior."

Terrence probably got the wrong impression from that statement. I took away my own authority as a teacher and as a person of Chinese descent when I handed the problem off to the white authority figure whom he was accustomed to seeing as having the power. It's not that I wanted to show Terrence how powerful I was or that I personally wanted to "get him back" for what he said; I merely realized that I was reinforcing a stereotype that he already had and resented about Asian Americans, that we are passive, and allow whites to have the power.

My guilt at mishandling the situation was further inflamed as I realized why I had handled the situation so passively: I was running away. I was running from the memory of being called "chink" and "ching chong fong." I was running as fast as I could away from the pain and the horror of those memories that flooded back into my mind of being ridiculed by my classmates. They would pull back their own eyelids and make slanty-eyed faces at me and each other pretending to speak Chinese. They said I ate dog food and that I smelled like Chinese takeout. The shame made me hate myself. I looked in the mirror and I would cry. I would put water on my face and try to rub out my image. I told my mother that I hated black hair and wanted to have blonde hair instead. I refused to bring lunch to school and bought hot lunch instead. I refused to speak Chinese for three years and purposely flunked out of Chinese school when I had been getting A's for months. I just told my mother I was American and couldn't possibly learn to read and write Chinese and that it was a dumb language anyway. For years and years, I hated myself because I was not accepted for who I was. I hated myself because other people's children had learned to hate, to mock, and to hurt those who did not look exactly like them. I know it may sound silly or overly dramatic, but I know that I have been scarred for life. I know this because I thought I had gotten past the shame. I re-embraced my cultural roots in late high school and in college. I was proud of who I was and didn't mind the image I saw in the mirror anymore. I even told myself I was pretty, despite not being blonde and blue eyed.

But after all those years of rebuilding my self-confidence, all it took to make me shake and hurt were those four little words, from an even littler boy—"You silly Chinese girl." It wasn't even a slur. He was stating a fact. I mean, I am a Chinese girl. His attitude was wrong, but then again, so was mine. Why hadn't I owned up to my heritage proudly right there in Ms. Sobel's classroom? Why hadn't I confronted Mrs. Tan or Terrence on my own? Why did I run away? It crushed me to see that I was still healing inside myself from those terrible elementary school experiences of racism. It crushed me even more that it was still happening to other children of minority status. I cried for me, for Terrence, for all the kids who were made to feel like nothing, like dirt, like aliens, like idiots just because they looked different. How does one conquer a monster that lives inside oneself? How does one teach others to respect differences, to embrace them and learn from them and share them without fear or prejudice?

Questions to Consider

1. How do you feel about the way the author responded to Terrence's comment? How would you have reacted? Have you ever been in a similar situation? Describe what was said and how you responded.

2. Terrence was described as going through a period of "*self-hate.*" What does that term mean to you? Have you ever had a student who has experienced "self-hate?" How did you know? Have you ever felt that way? Describe your feelings and how it affected you.

3. The author changes her mind about how she responded to Terrence after hearing about his behavior at home. Why?

4. Have you ever been made fun of, or made fun of someone else in school? Describe one situation in which a student made fun of you, or in which you made fun of another person. Try to describe how both sides were feeling during the incident (you might have to guess at what the other person was feeling).

5. The author asks several questions at the end of her narrative. Choose one or two and try to answer them:
   • Why hadn't I owned up to my heritage proudly right there in Ms. Sobel's classroom?
   • Why hadn't I confronted Mrs. Tan or Terrence on my own?
   • Why did I run away?
   • How does one conquer a monster that lives inside oneself?
   • How does one teach others to respect differences, to embrace them and learn from them and share them without fear or prejudice?

NARRATIVE 5

Before You Read

What does it mean to be white? Black? Asian? Think about your race (or races) and try to list all of the characteristics that form your racial identity. Which of these characteristics are physical in nature and thus visible to others? Which one are not? How does being white/black/Asian affect your relationship with your students? Do students respect you more, less, or the same due to your racial group membership?

White on the Outside

I began my career teaching first grade in a public school in the Baltimore City School District. Although I knew that the school I was teaching in was 93 percent African American and 7 percent Caucasian before I started, I had no idea all of the implications that could hold. And with a staff of about 75 percent African American, as a white person I was glaringly a minority everywhere I went.

When the girls and boys came rushing in on that first day I was so delighted to finally meet them! This was the class I would spend the next nine months with and I had been preparing for it all summer! I had high expectations for a fun and productive year.

As the year progressed we all got to know each other and the classroom routines. Everything seemed to be running smoothly until one day, Dylan, one of my black students, approached me, seemingly upset. He said that another student had called him white. I asked him why that bothered him so much and he said that he was not white, he was black. He went on to say that he would never want to be white and doesn't want the other children to think he is. I asked him if it was bad to be white and he looked at me and responded in an obvious tone, "Yeah."

I told him that I was white and upon hearing this he, and a couple other nearby students, chuckled. "Oh, Miss Costa, you're not white—you're just light-skinned and that's okay!" said Lois. I took this opportunity to have a dialogue with the students about race. I told them that indeed I was white and that this is not good or bad, just different. Several children told me that their parents, older siblings, or friends had told them that being white was certainly a bad thing. They continued to tell me not to get upset and that being light-skinned is okay. Despite my efforts to convince them of my color, they would not hear of it.

The year progressed but the dynamics of our room had changed. I had learned that to my students being white is unfavorable, and although at the beginning of the year they clearly understood that I was white, at this point the children believed me to be black, just like them. They had an image of whites disrespecting them. I felt that because they began to trust and respect me, and because they knew that I trusted and respected them, they thought I must be black. So, instead of trying to understand that whites and blacks can be equal, they simply forced themselves into believing that I was black; a much easier transition in thinking for a six year old.

I ended up looping with my children to second grade and so continued the fantasy that I was black. As the year went on and my students would not believe me when I told them the truth about my race, I began to feel discouraged. I did not want these children to perpetuate the idea that their parents and community had passed on to them. I wanted them to know that kindness, camaraderie, honesty, and other character traits to do not depend on a person's race, that color does not determine a person's entire being. I wanted them to understand that I was white. But dialogues, activities, and even having the children meet my parents did not seem to get the message across.

On the last day of second grade, after being with my students for two years, I sat them down and explained to them that I would be leaving the school to go to graduate school and I wanted them to know one last thing about me. I told them that I knew we'd discussed this before but this time it was important that they believe me. I said to them, quite simply, "I am white." They could tell my tone was sullen and serious. They could tell that this meant a lot to me. And they just sat quietly on the carpet mulling over what they finally knew to be the truth. When one boy, Trian, finally spoke he said to me, with the approval of all the other students, "Miss Costa, you may be white on the outside, but you black on the inside."

I carry that comment around with me, not knowing how to feel about it. Not knowing whether the children ever understood, or ever will understand, that being white to them does equal being mean or hurtful or being a bad teacher. Part of me feels I should be flattered and accept what Trian said as the compliment he intended it to be, but part of me wishes that those students could simply understand.

Questions to Consider

1. Why do you think that Dylan was so upset to be called white? What made it "bad" to be white? Why do you think that Dylan felt this way? How might he have learned this idea?

2. What does the statement, "You're not white—you're just light-skinned," mean in the context of the story? In your experience, what value is placed on skin color in the white community? The black community? The Asian community?

3. Why do you think the students were so invested in the idea that their teacher was not white? How did it make them feel to think that she might be white? Do you think that the author's hypothesis, "because they knew that I trusted and respected them, I must be black," is valid? Why or why not?

4. Why do you think it was so important for the teacher to convince her students that she is white? Would you have tried to do the same? Why or why not?

5. Trian's comment to his teacher, "You may be white on the outside, but you black on the inside," contains an example of Ebonics, or African American Vernacular English (AAVE), in the omission of the word *are* in "you (are) black on the inside." How does reading that sentence in print make you

feel? How do you feel when you hear Ebonics spoken in school? In the street? On television or in movies?

6. What does it mean to be "white on the outside, black on the inside" (or vice versa)? What do the terms "Uncle Tom" or "Oreo cookie" mean? When is it considered a good thing to be one race on the outside but another on the inside? When is it bad? Why?

Project and Extension Activities

1. Look at the cartoon at the start of this chapter. List the racial stereotypes presented by the two characters. Have you ever heard statements of this nature before? How do they make you feel as you read them? Do you believe any of them to be true? If so, which ones? What is the race of the two characters in this cartoon? Does the identity of the characters have an effect on the acceptability of the comments? What makes you think so? Create a cartoon in which two characters talk about some of the stereotypes that exist about your own race or ethnicity.

2. Read this method of addressing prejudiced statements:

An example: Why would a talented and well-educated teacher like you choose to work in a neighborhood like that? Aren't most of your students African American (Asian American, Hispanic American, Native American or any group experiencing discrimination)?

1. Pull the prejudice out of the comment and restate it in a calm and objective way.
   Many people seem to think that African American (Asian American, Hispanic American, Native American) children, particularly if they live in disadvantaged communities, are less capable.
2. State personal beliefs in a clear and assertive manner.
   I have always acted on my own belief that every child is filled with potential and deserves the finest possible education.
3. Make a positive statement about the specific subjects of the prejudice.
   If you visited my classroom, you might be surprised to see how intelligent and successful my children really are. In fact, you might even want to visit sometime.
4. Gently turn the subject to a new direction.
   Do you still travel into the city frequently for your work?

Can you see yourself using this method? Why or why not? Try this over the course of a week. Keep a log of your interactions. In which instances did it work? In which instances didn't it work? Why do you think it did or did not help the situation?

3. Look at the following cartoon. To whom is the girl referring when she says "I hate them too"? What do you think the boy might have said to elicit such a response? If there were another frame in the cartoon, how do you think the boy might have responded to the girl's statement? Design another frame to "finish" the cartoon and compare your ending to that of a partner.

Copyright © Daryl Cagle, Cagle Cartoons, Inc. Reprinted by permission.

4. Advertisements are aimed to appeal to specific demographic groups. Advertisers will create different versions of ads for different magazines, depending on the audience of the publication.

Choose two magazines aimed at different racial or ethnic groups and compare their advertisements. Choose two ads (one from each magazine) for the same product or from the same manufacturer and answer these questions:
• How do you know to which group the ad is geared?
• What are the desired results for each ad?
• What are some of the underlying feelings behind the attraction of each ad for the reader?
• What might the reader try to achieve by buying the products depicted in each ad?

Show the ad to a friend or classmate. Ask them to guess the target audience and magazine or newspaper of origin.

5. In the beginning of this chapter, we addressed the problematic nature of assigning to students the task of creating a family tree. Not only do many students have trouble with researching their family tree, but so do many teachers. Try to trace your own family tree and then answer the following questions:
   - Was it easy or difficult to complete your tree?
   - Did the project cause you any problems? What sort of problems did the project present for you?
   - Would it cause any of your students trouble? If so, which students and why?

   Now think of an alternative to the family tree project that all your students could successfully complete. One possibility is an "important people quilt" in which the people who are most important to the students each have one square. This allows children to celebrate nonfamily members, caregivers, and other people who are influential in their lives. Try your alternative project yourself or with a group of students.

6. Stereotypical portrayals of different racial or ethnic groups on television are numerous and often offensive. Choose one "offending" TV show and analyze the portrayal of a specific character that you feel is stereotypically represented. Answer the following questions:
   - What group(s) is this character intended to represent?
   - What does the character *do* that makes her or him representative of the group?
   - How does the character *look* that makes him or her representative of the group?
   - In what ways in the character funny? Successful? Intelligent? What are her or his dominant characteristics?
   - Do you like this character? Why or why not?

   Now interview a member of the representative group about the character. (Note: your interviewee should have seen the same TV show and be somewhat familiar with the character.) Ask the following questions:
   - Is this character a valid representation of your culture/group? If yes, in what ways? If no, why not?
   - Do you feel that this character has brought positive or negative attention to your group? Why?
   - If you were given the keys to the TV studio for a day, and were able to create a show about your culture/group, what would your main character be like?

7. Conduct action research in your school, or by visiting a different school. Be a "fly on the wall" by observing the use of racial and ethnic epithets during a period of one school day. Count the number of times that students use racial or ethnic terms in school. You might want to choose different locations for your research (i.e., the school cafeteria, the hallways, the playground, the classroom). Report information about the actors (gender and race/ethnicity) and their intent for these words in terms of negative, positive, or neutral meaning. Record whether there was any adult intervention. Document your observations using a chart such as the following:

Term	Location	Meaning	Intervention	Actors
spic	cafeteria	negative	teacher reprimand	one white girl aimed at one Hispanic girl
nigger	hallway	positive	none	two black boys

What do you notice about the places where racial/ethnic name calling most frequently takes place? Where is there the most intervention from adults? What labels are viewed as negative? Positive? Neutral? When do adults intervene, and how do they do so? Does anything surprise you about the use of this language by students?

Cultural Exploration

1. *Explore neighborhoods:* Visit a neighborhood that is predominately inhabited by one race or ethnic group. If possible, go accompanied by a member of that race/ethnic group. Create an annotated map about your exploration. Include the places you visited, photos or memorabilia where possible, and brief descriptions or reactions to each site. Address the following questions:
   - What physical signs are there that indicate which race/group lives in that area?
   - What linguistic cues (in verbal speech) do you hear? How did you communicate with the community on your visit?
   - What cultural centers do you see?
   - How are people dressed? Is the clothing similar to or different from your own?
   - What type of food is available? Do people eat on the street? In restaurants? In homes?
   - What religious institutions (if any) are present?
   - How do people gather? (e.g., in small groups, pairs, alone?)

   Discuss how your visit made you feel. Use the following continua to start thinking about your interaction with the neighborhood. (Note: Use the terms as ends of a continuum rather than as dyadic opposites. It is more likely that you would feel varying degrees of both descriptors at different points in your exploration.)

   Did you feel comfortable <---> uncomfortable?
   Did you feel included <---> excluded?
   Were you interested <---> disinterested?

2. *Explore people:* Interview a member of an ethnic or racial group. Address the following questions:
   - What does it mean to you to be a member of the _____ (racial/ethnic group) community?
   - Do you feel a strong affiliation with your race/ethnic group? In what ways? In which ways not?
   - Did you ever experience racism or prejudice because of your group membership? Describe.
   - How does being a member of your group affect the way you view the world?

     Using the answers to these and other questions from your interview, write a brief biography of the person. Share the bio with your interviewee and ask for feedback as to its accuracy. (Note: As with most everything else regarding issues of culture and identity, please remember that your interviewee's responses will be individual and subjective, and will not necessarily reflect the feelings of an entire race or ethnic group.)

3. *Explore literature:* Choose to read about a race/ethnicity that interests you, or one about which you have questions.

Novels, Short Stories, Memoirs: choose one

- *Invisible Man,* Ralph Ellison
- *The Autobiography of Malcolm X,* Alex Haley
- *The Bluest Eye,* Toni Morrison
- *I Know Why the Caged Bird Sings,* Maya Angelou
- *Are Italians White?,* Jennifer Guglielmo & Salvatore Salerno
- *Paper Daughter,* Elaine Mar
- *Interpreter of Maladies,* Jhumpa Lahiri
- *The House on Mango Street,* Sandra Cisneros
- *Growing up Latino: Memoirs and Stories,* Harold Augenbaum & Ilan Stavans, Eds.
- *A Border Passage: From Cairo to America—A Woman's Journey,* Leila Ahmed
- *Double Loyalties: South Asian Adolescents in the West,* Paul A. Singh Ghuman

Young Adult Literature: choose two

- *Half and Half: Writers on Growing Up Biracial and Bicultural,* Claudine C. O'Hearn
- *What Are You? Voices of Mixed-Race Young People,* Pearl Fuyo Gaskins
- *On the Rez,* Ian Frazier
- *Island of Blue Dolphins,* Scott O'Dell
- *A White Romance,* Virginia Hamilton
- *Necessary Roughness,* Marie G. Lee

- *Yell-Oh Girls: Emerging Voices Explore Culture, Identity, and Growing up Asian American,* Vicki Nam
- *American Dragons: Twenty-Five Asian American Voices,* Laurence Yep
- *From the Notebooks of Melanin Sun,* Jacqueline Woodson
- *Zack,* William Bell
- *Born Confused,* Tanuja Hidier
- *Angelfish,* Laurence Yep

Picturebooks: Choose three

- *Under Our Skin: Kids Talk About Race,* Debbie Holsclaw Birdseye
- *How Tía Lola Came to Visit/Stay,* Julia Alvarez
- *In My Family/En mi familia,* Carmen Lomas Garza
- *Jalapeño Bagels,* Natasha Wing
- *Building a Bridge,* Lisa Shook Begaye
- *The Story of Ruby Bridges,* Robert Coles
- *Father's Rubber Shoes,* Yumi Heo
- *Dia's Story Cloth,* Dia Cha
- *The Name Jar,* Yangsook Choi
- *Char Siu Bao Boy,* Sandra Yamate
- *Two Mrs. Gibsons,* Toyomi Igus
- *Skin Again,* bell hooks
- *Indian Shoes,* Cynthia Leitich Mith & Jim Madsen
- *The Colors of Us,* Karen Katz

Write a reaction to the literature you have chosen. Address the following questions:
- What were your thoughts about the culture(s) before your reading?
- Did those thoughts change after your reading? If so, how?
- Did you learn anything new about the culture? What, if anything, surprised you?

 Internet Connection

Polyethnic.com

An excellent website devoted to discussion of diversity and ethnicity. Read four award-winning student essays or visit a page with specific information about the following ethnicities: Native, African, German, British, Asian, Russian, Italian, Irish, Arab, and Latino.
http://www.polyethnic.com

The Foundation for Ethnic Understanding

One of the main goals of this organization is to "foster face-to-face dialog between ethnic communities." Click on the "publications" link to download the "Shared Dreams" high school student curriculum guide in PDF format. View a list of current initiatives and get involved in a campaign or project.
http://www.ffeu.org

Rethinking Schools Online

An online version of the magazine devoted to "equity and to the vision that public education is central to the creation of a humane, caring, multiracial democracy." Some articles are available to read in the archives. Click on "Publications" for a list of books and other materials (of particular interest are back issues of the excellent publication *Rethinking our Classrooms*). Visit the "Just for Fun" link at the top of the page for games, maps, and quizzes.
http://www.rethinkingschools.org

Diversity Works

Dedicated to peer diversity education and helping youth "expand their understanding of power and oppression" through educational workshops, projects, and community events. Visit this site for a model of specific ideas about how to work with students in your own school community.
http://www.diversityworks.org

The Prejudice Institute

"Devoted to policy research and education on all dimensions of prejudice, discrimination, and ethnoviolence." Click on the "Factsheets" tab for information about such subjects as ethnoviolence, skinheads, and Arab Americans. There is also a good Action Sheet entitled "What Teenagers Can Do About Prejudice."
http://www.prejudiceinstitute.org

Applied Research Center

The Center is a "public policy, educational and research institute whose work emphasizes issues of race and social change." Read selected excerpts from the online archives of the journal *ColorLines*. Of particular interest is the J.U.M.P. (Justice is the Unifying Message) project that works to address "civil liberties, racial profiling, and human rights abuses." Click on publications for curricula and toolkits.
http://www.arc.org/

References and Recommended Reading

Apple, M. W. (1990). *Ideology and curriculum.* New York: Routledge.

Arboleda, T. (1998). *In the shadow of race: Growing up as a multiethnic, multicultural, and "multiracial" American.* Mahwah, NJ: Lawrence Erlbaum Associates.

Banks, J. A. (2003). *Teaching strategies for ethnic studies.* Boston: Allyn & Bacon.

Carter, R., & Goodwin, A. L. (1994). Racial identity and education. In L. Darling-Hammond (Ed.), *Review of research in education* (Vol. 20, pp. 291–336). Washington, DC: American Educational Research Association.

Delpit, L. (1995). *Other people's children: Cultural conflict in the classroom.* New York: New Press.

Espinoza-Herold, M. (2003). *Issues in Latino education: Race, school culture, and the politics of academic success.* Boston: Allyn & Bacon.

Fennimore, B. S. (1994). Addressing prejudiced statements: A four-step method that works! *Childhood Education, 70*(4), 202–204.

Freire, P. (2003). *Pedagogy of the oppressed.* New York: Continuum.

Gordon, E. W. (1999). *Education and justice: A view from the back of the bus.* New York: Teachers College Press.

Hernández Sheets, R., & Hollins, E. (Eds.). (1999). *Racial and ethnic identity in school practices.* Mahwah, NJ: Lawrence Erlbaum Associates.

hooks, bell. (1995). *Killing rage, ending racism.* New York: Henry Holt & Co.

hooks, bell. (1994). *Teaching to transgress: Education as the practice of freedom.* New York: Routledge.

Howard, G. R. (1999). *We can't teach what we don't know: White teachers, multiracial schools.* New York: Teachers College Press.

Jones, T. G., & Fuller, M. (2003). *Teaching Hispanic children.* Boston: Allyn & Bacon.

McCarthy, C., & Crichlow, W. (Eds.). (1993). *Race, identity, and representation in education.* New York: Routledge.

Ogbu, J. (1994). Race stratification and education in the United States: Why inequality persists. *TC Record, 96*(2), 264–298.

Ogbu, J., & Davis, A. (2003). *Black American students in an affluent suburb: A study of academic disengagement.* Mahwah, NJ: Lawrence Erlbaum Associates.

Paley, V. G. (1989). *White teacher.* Cambridge, MA: Harvard University Press.

Pollock, M. (2004). *Colormute: Race talk dilemmas in an American school.* Princeton, NJ: Princeton University Press.

Shimahara, N. K., Holowinsky, I. Z., & Tomlinson-Clarke, S. (Eds.). (2001). *Ethnicity, race, and nationality in education: A global perspective.* Mahwah, NJ: Lawrence Erlbaum Associates.

Swindker Boutte, G. (Ed.). (2002). *Resounding voices: School experiences of people from diverse ethnic backgrounds.* Boston: Allyn & Bacon.

Taylor, L. S. (2003). *Bridging multiple worlds: Case studies of diverse educational communities.* Boston: Allyn & Bacon.

Teaching Tolerance. (1997). *Starting small: Teaching tolerance in preschool and the early grades.* Montgomery, AL: Southern Poverty Law Center.

Waters, M. C. (1990). *Ethnic options: Choosing identities in America.* Berkeley: CA: University of California Press.

Watkins, W. H., Lewis, J. H., & Chou, V. (Eds.). (2001). *Race and education: The roles of history and society in educating African-American students.* Boston: Allyn & Bacon.

Weinberg, M. (1997). *Asian-American education: Historical background and current realities.* Mahwah, NJ: Lawrence Erlbaum Associates.

Wong, S. C. (1993). Promises, pitfalls and the principles of text selection in curricular diversification. In T. Perry & J. Fraser (Eds.), *Freedom's plow* (pp. 109–120). New York: Routledge.

Learning Styles

A Place to Begin

We've all experienced classes that, simply put, bored us to tears. Thankfully, we are sure to have experienced those that had us riveted to our seats as well. Often these differences correlate with our personal tastes and interests in different subjects. However, it can also have to do with our learning style or, what Gardner (1983, 1999) calls our "multiple intelligences."

We all learn in different ways. While some may prefer to receive information through visual stimuli, others may need to hear information to process it efficiently and effectively. To better understand diversity in terms of learning styles, let's examine some of the main theories.

Harvard educator and theorist Howard Gardner (1983) coined the term *multiple intelligences* to refer to the diversity of intelligences that humans exhibit. His original theory described seven distinct intelligences:

1. *Linguistic*—facility with oral and written language, ability to learn languages, use language to express oneself, and as a way of remembering information
2. *Logical/mathematical*—ability to do scientific investigations, logic problems, and mathematical operations
3. *Musical*—ability to perform, compose, and analyze music as well as a facility with recognizing musical tone, rhythms, and pitch
4. *Bodily/kinesthetic*—facility with body movements, ability to coordinate mind and body to solve problems
5. *Spatial*—ability to recognize patterns both in space and in confined areas
6. *Interpersonal*—ability to work well with people, to interpret intentions, motivations, and desires
7. *Intrapersonal*—facility in understanding one's own desires, feelings, and motivations

After the success of his original theory, Gardner (1999) added three more intelligences:

8. *Naturalist*—facility in recognizing, categorizing, and utilizing one's environment
9. *Spiritual/existential*—Gardner sees this intelligence as possibly problematic with regard to the "content" of spiritual intelligence, believing that an interest in and understanding of religious and spiritual matters may be one element of existential intelligence, which would be an ability to consider the "big questions" of life
10. *Moral*—"a concern with those rules, behaviors and attitudes that govern the sanctity of life" (1999, p. 70).

Of these three new intelligences, Gardner claims that naturalist intelligence properly belongs with the original seven. The last two—spiritual/existential intelligence and moral intelligence—are more controversial, and are still being researched.

It is important to remember that, although these intelligences are presented as individual entities, they in fact exist and work in conjunction with each other, each one supporting the other. So, for example, someone who might be said to have strong linguistic intelligence, likely also exhibits some logical/mathematical intelligence as well. The intelligences are not isolated units, but rather intersect and are interrelated. The mind is a system whose parts are not separable.

Gardner suggests that in schools we are most interested in the first two intelligences, linguistic and logical/mathematical, and thus emphasize, praise, and reward students the most for displaying these abilities. Gardner's theory offers us the means to discover new ways of teaching students by reaching the full spectrum of intelligences.

Since students come to the educational table with a variety of intelligences, it makes sense to look at the ways in which we teach through the lens of these intelligences as well. Look at this chart that describes several different styles of teaching:

Intelligence	Teaching Activities (examples)	Teaching Materials (examples)	Instructional Strategies
Linguistic	lectures, discussions, word games, storytelling, choral reading, journal writing, etc.	books, tape recorders, type-writers, stamp sets, books on tape, etc.	read about it, write about it, talk about it, listen to it
Logical-Mathematical	brain teasers, problem solving, science experiments, mental calculation, number games, critical thinking, etc.	calculators, math manipulatives, science equipment, math games, etc.	quantify it, think critically about it, conceptualize it
Spatial	visual presentations, art activities, imagination games, mind-mapping, metaphor, visualization, etc.	graphs, maps, video, LEGO sets, art materials, optical illusions, cameras, picture library, etc.	see it, draw it, visualize it, color it, mind-map it,
Bodily-Kinesthetic	hands-on learning, drama, dance, sports that teach, tactile activities, relaxation exercises, etc.	building tools, clay, sports equipment, manipulatives, tactile learning resources, etc.	build it, act it out, touch it, get a "gut feeling" of it, dance it
Musical	superlearning, rapping, songs that teach	tape recorder, tape collection, musical instruments	sing it, rap it, listen to it

Interpersonal	cooperative learning, peer tutoring, community involvement, social gatherings, simulations, etc.	board games, party supplies, props for role plays, etc.	teach it, collaborate on it, interact with respect to it
Intrapersonal	individualized instruction, independent study, options in course of study, self-esteem building,etc.	self-checking materials, journals, materials for projects, etc.	connect it to your personal life, make choices with regard to it
Linguistic	Whole Language	teaching through storytelling	long word on the blackboard
Logical-Mathematical	Critical Thinking	Socratic questioning	posing a logical paradox
Spatial	Integrated Arts Instruction	drawing/mind-mapping concepts	unusual picture on the overhead
Bodily-Kinesthetic	Hands-On Learning dramatic expressions	using gestures/	mysterious artifact passed around the class
Musical	Suggestopedia	using voice rhythmically	piece of music played as students come into class into class
Interpersonal	Cooperative Learning	dynamically interacting with students	"Turn to a neighbor and share . . ."
Intrapersonal	Individualized Instruction	bringing *feeling* into presentation	"Close your eyes and think of a time in your life when . . ."

Look through the activities, materials, and strategies listed. Which style do you think best describes your own teaching? Think about some of educational movements that are embraced by your school. Which intelligences are being validated by these methodologies?

Learning styles are similar to intelligences in that they describe a way in which a person interprets information. While we might be inclined to deem this one's "preference," it is far more a cognitive strength than a choice for students. For example, if you are a visual learner, you might be tempted to say "I prefer to learn with pictures rather than text." However, it is more likely that you learn more efficiently and thoroughly with images than through reading or hearing information. (Reading of course does involve vision, but is categorized separately due to its emphasis on linguistic abilities.) This is your learning style, not merely a taste for visual information.

There are three major learning styles. (There are also others, which space does not permit us to discuss here. For a good overview, see Mamchur [1996]):

- *Visual*—learns best by seeing information presented graphically or pictorially
- *Auditory*—learns best by hearing information
- *Tactile/kinesthetic*—learns best by touching, doing, and moving one's body

Given the fact that we, as learners, all have different styles and intelligences, it is only logical to think that as teachers, we bring these intelligences into the classroom and into our teaching. If we are tactile/kinesthetic learners, we might be more likely to plan lessons that involve movement and hands-on experiences. Understanding one's own learning style, teaching style, and types of intelligence is the first step to designing more varied lessons. Understanding our students' diversity in learning styles will help us to think more broadly about our curriculum and how it is transmitted in our class, our school, and our communities.

NARRATIVE 6

Before You Read

Think about students in your class or school that simply do not "play by the rules." They may not follow directions or do things in a "traditional" way. Perhaps one solves math problems correctly, but not the way the teacher taught the steps. Perhaps another categorizes written information in terms of the mental images he gets from it, rather than by the actual words used. How are these students alike? How are they different? How are these students treated by teachers? Is their creativity rewarded or punished? In which circumstances are their abilities praised? When are they criticized? Do they do well on exams and quizzes? Oral assessments? Performances?

How do you solve problems? Do you read the instructions and follow a set pattern of steps? Do you try to solve a problem without any guidance? How do you feel when you solve a problem without having followed the prescribed steps? Do you feel that it is okay to do things differently? Why or why not?

Think about your students' social interactions. Do some students seem to have more friends than others? To what do you attribute their popularity? And the students who have few friends? To what do you attribute their "lack" of popularity?

Doing School Her Own Way

This parenting business is not easy. In my years of being a mom, I have found two milestones to be extremely difficult. The first was when my daughter developed her own opinions—about everything. The second was the beginning of school, of the formal education years.

Many parents and caregivers look forward to the latter for reasons ranging from a need for some time alone to respect for the value of and need for education. I fall into this second category. However, my years as a student and as a teacher myself had not prepared me to experience school from a parent's viewpoint.

Let me take a moment to emphasize that I do not belong to the "not my child" mentality. I know that my daughter makes mistakes, is not always honest, and actually may be doing some or many of the things about which the teachers complain. I also understand that teachers have many students, necessary regulations, and overwhelming work requirements. Still, my daughter is the most important child in the world to me—and I watched as our school system slowly destroyed her.

Schools have a public and a private face. The public face makes reference to highly educated professionals who receive quality, supplemental staff development and who tailor the curriculum to meet each student's needs, and to the importance of the home connection and parental involvement.

The other face of public education, the "hidden curriculum," emphasizes numbers— scores on standardized tests by which the schools and principals are judged. It also places a high value on following the rules. This reality forms the cracks through which too many children, including my daughter, fall.

My daughter, Wendy, is the product of the NYC public school system in the 1990s. Her elementary classes averaged 25 pupils. Her teachers were mostly seasoned veterans. Her fellow students were generally considered middle class.

Gardner's ideas on multiple learning styles are popular with many teachers. They understand that some children are visual learners, while others rely on more auditory or kinesthetic approaches. While research has demonstrated that a majority of elementary school teachers have weak backgrounds in mathematical concepts and processes, my daughter demonstrates a high degree of logical/mathematical intelligence. She was able to answer questions correctly, but didn't follow the prescribed steps for solving problems.

Teachers just didn't "get" my daughter and the way her mind worked. They did not appreciate her alternative ways of doing math and even took issue with some of her questions. They saw her as unusual; and when your teacher thinks you're unusual, or reacts differently to you than to other children, the other students pick up these cues.

Right from the start, Wendy's kindergarten teacher noticed differences. Wendy often chose puzzles, mazes, and measuring activities, unlike most of the other girls in the class. She intervened in other children's fights, exhibiting a strong sense of fair play, and stood up for victims. When the teacher gave directions, Wendy frequently questioned them, suggesting other options. This last trait got her thrown out of dance class at age 5!

Formal math and science instruction began in the first grade. Oh, the phone calls! "Your daughter's questions are making it hard for me to teach the other children."

"Sometimes, Wendy acts like she knows more than I do." How does one respond to these statements? If you told me she was violent, or ignoring her work, or a host of other possibilities, I could pull out my bag of tricks. But Wendy would come home and show me her teachers' approaches and darn it, sometimes that little kid really had ideas that made more sense—especially in math. We tried therapy, but what was the actual problem?

A few years later, we realized the actual problem: no one likes a showoff, even if that was never Wendy's intent. She was just trying to make sense of the world, particularly the world of school, in her own mathematical terms. But the other children picked up on her teachers' verbal and nonverbal responses, and Wendy became the unpopular class nerd.

I had many opportunities to observe Wendy at school and on class trips. I saw teachers becoming increasingly annoyed by her questions and alternate approaches to assignments. I listened to the conversations her classmates engaged in—things Wendy could care less about such as clothing, hairstyles, gossip, or sports. When she tried to talk about things going on in class, or ideas that interested her, children moved away from her. After a few trips, no one asked her to join them on the bus, or to walk in their group. Instead of helping the situation by assigning seats and groups, the teachers turned a blind eye.

Parents know that childhood illnesses happen. They realize that their children need help with schoolwork. But what do they know about what is truly most important to their children—social interaction and acceptance? Where is that focused on in school? What part of the day is allotted for appreciating the differences in each individual, for character education and development? Wendy had reached the point where she lost her social confidence.

Although literacy, with all of its reading and writing aspects, is a major educational goal, what about "social literacy?" Where is the recognition in school of the true impact of social relations and their lack? Shouldn't professional development workshops for educators also consider this extremely important topic?

Fast forward to high school. Social patterns developed in elementary school continued. Math and science classes began to have real depth, something Wendy could truly appreciate. And still, she disagreed with some of her teachers, created her own formulas and equations, questioned more and more. Her teachers didn't appreciate her, or rise to her challenges, or communicate anything personally. They reacted negatively, and Wendy was once again basically ostracized by her classmates. Her inability to relate to her own age group became even worse.

Wendy continued to seek out older friends. She had finally gotten the message that her interests were not shared by many people her age. In high school, the only crowd that would accept her was a group that didn't do a lot of talking. I don't even want to discuss what this group was into doing, but it was neither healthy nor always legal.

There's no happy ending to this parent's story yet. Wendy quit high school after skipping her junior year, devastated by her peers' and teachers' reactions to her. Without opening a book, she took the GED exam and received 97 percent and higher in every subject, but quit college after a single term. She had no idea how to relate to or deal with her teachers or other students. It didn't have to be this way. Elementary school, the early years, are not just about academics. Anyone who thinks that they are should come meet Wendy.

Questions to Consider

1. The author refers to the "private and public face" of education. Do you agree with this characterization? Why or why not?
2. Wendy's mother describes her as exhibiting logical/mathematical intelligence. Based on what you read, with which of Gardner's seven original intelligences do you think Wendy struggles? What evidence supports your thoughts?
3. Why do you think Wendy's teachers felt uncomfortable with her alternative ways of doing math? Have you ever been in a similar situation?
4. Wendy's mother describes her daughter questioning the teacher. Do you think it is appropriate for students to question the teacher during class? Why or why not? Has this ever happened to you? How did you respond?
5. The author states, "When your teacher thinks you're unusual, or reacts differently to you than to other children, the other students pick up these cues." Do you agree with this statement? Why or why not? What role do the teacher's interactions with students play in each student's social life in school? Why do you think Wendy's classmates reacted negatively towards her?
6. What might her teachers have done to include Wendy more in the classroom community? What would you have done?

NARRATIVE 7

Before You Read

As teachers we have all met these students: very bright, highly creative, yet unmotivated in the traditional sense. They do not do homework, study for tests, or follow through on class projects. Still, they understand the material and may even know more than what has been taught in class. Despite their intelligence, many teachers are still uncomfortable with these students' work ethic.

Think about a student or students in your school that match this description. Are they successful or unsuccessful in terms of academic and school culture (i.e., get good grades, pass tests, avoid trouble)? What are their strengths? Weaknesses? How do these strengths/weaknesses affect their performance in class?

No Homework, Please

From a motivational standpoint, I didn't come to understand why homework was assigned to students until I reached college. Success for me as a high school student was defined by my understanding of the subject matter and internalizing it to a point where it was relevant to me and I could understand why I should care. Homework (and I specifically mean that type that involves repetitive practice exercises) did not generally help me to this end, or so I thought at the time. For the most part,

I was able to make my way through high school by attending every class and paying attention to the lessons. I did the assigned homework half of the time, at most, and still found myself adequately prepared for tests and quizzes.

There is one instance in particular that stands apart from the rest in my early academic career: a Spanish class that I took during my sophomore year. It was a great class, but one I almost failed. The lecture time was complemented with videos in Spanish, as well as other activities that helped the subject matter become more meaningful and natural. There were tons of different magazines and newspapers in the classroom from Spanish-speaking countries, and assignments regularly involved reading these.

Not only did we have lessons on the subjunctive mood but we also learned about holidays and beliefs of Spanish-speaking people. I felt that not only was I learning the mechanics of the Spanish language but I was also being immersed in the cultures of the Spanish-speaking world.

My teacher assigned daily homework and checked it every day at the beginning of class. The homework grade weighed heavily on the final semester grade so that, regardless of how well one understood the material, a student barely got away without doing the work. This should have been enough to encourage me to do homework, but it wasn't. Time after time, I would come away from class feeling like I had understood the material and was ready to take the test. All I had to do was listen to the lesson and I was able to internalize the vocabulary, the grammar, or the information. When tests came I did do well, but I was still not passing the class because I wasn't doing the homework. I would rationalize this behavior by asking myself, Why should I practice verb conjugations for an hour when I had already learned it during class and could remember it for a test at the end of the week?

When the teacher and I spoke about this situation, she made me a deal: If I could keep up the quiz and test grades, attend every class, and pay attention, I didn't have to do the homework. Needless to say, this was what I had been waiting to hear all my life! The class went on and I did fine on the tests and quizzes. It was only mildly embarrassing when I would be skipped over as the teacher came through and checked everyone else's homework. While I don't recall exactly what grade I received in the end, I do remember that it was in the A or B range, but would not have been so high without our special deal.

Having gone through college and become a teacher myself, I look back on this episode with mixed feelings—not because it was so definitive on its own but for what it symbolized about my general development as a student. My first year and a half of college was very difficult for me. I went to a very competitive school where my high school work ethic just did not cut it. I encountered peers who handled much more material than simply what was covered during lecture time. My grades suffered to the point where I almost withdrew. It took about a year to relearn such essentials as notetaking skills, researching skills, and the value of practice on my time so that I could come to class with questions and homework ready.

Now whenever I take a class, I take extensive notes and do all the assigned homework, and I review my work as well. The lessons that I learned are not so easy to explain to graduate schools when they inquire what happened to my grades in college. It is a problem that I have overcome, but that still haunts me. Should my teachers have been stricter on me in high school? Would it have worked, or would it just have made things worse?

Questions to Consider

1. How would you define the narrator's learning style? How was he so successful on exams and quizzes without doing the homework?
2. Based on the narrator's description of his Spanish class, how would you describe the teacher's teaching style? Did it seem to be working for the narrator? For which students might this style *not* work?
3. Do you agree with the deal made by the teacher and student not to do the homework? Would you have made such a deal? Why or why not? What kind of homework policy do you have in your school? In your class?
4. Why didn't the narrator's learning style work for him in college? How did he have to change to succeed?
5. The narrator is now a teacher himself. How do you think his own teaching style has developed?
6. The narrator ends his narrative with two questions: "Should my teachers have been stricter on me in high school? Would it have worked, or would it just have made things worse?" How would you answer his questions?

Project and Extension Activities

1. Look at these two cartoons:

"I think I'm beginning to grasp the concept of infinity."

Copyright © 1992 by Nick Downes. Reprinted by permission.

How would you describe each teacher's style of teaching? What type of student might benefit from each? Pretend that you are the chairperson of the Science Department at your school. Write a "want ad" for the type of teacher you would like to teach science. Give specific details about how that teacher should plan lessons, design projects, and conduct classes.

2. Visit one of the following websites and take a learning styles survey:
   - *http://www.ldpride.net/learning_style.html*
   - *http://library.cuesta.cc.ca.us/distance/lrnstyle.htm*
   - *http://www.nd.edu/~learning/styles/LTS.html*

- *http://www.studyguide.org/learning_styles.htm*
- *http://www.engr.ncsu.edu/learningstyles/ilsweb.html*

What is your learning style? Does the answer surprise you? Write about one school incident that reflects your learning style.

3. Have your students take a learning style inventory on one of the sites listed in Activity 2. Create a list of your students' preferred learning styles. Keep this list in your gradebook or next to your lesson plans.

4. Do action research in your classroom. Videotape a lesson or a period of your teaching day. Analyze the footage by observing yourself and then your students. Which learning style characterizes your teaching? Create a graph depicting the styles you most employ and the percentage of time you use each style in your lesson. Which students seem to be connecting to your style? Which don't? How can you tell?

5. Read this short narrative from a high school student:

"This year, as a sophomore, I had a bad experience with a social studies teacher. On the first day of class I knew that this teacher was a direct product of college. I mean, she had a lot of educational sense (she was very smart), but not a lot of common sense. She started out the class by making contradictory comments as she handed out our textbooks. 'I don't really like these textbooks because they have too many pictures and not enough words,' she said to her astounded students. She continued: 'You will get an assignment from them almost every night.' If you ask me, that statement just sounded stupid. If she didn't approve of them, why would she make us use them every night? That's just busy work, and busy work is the teacher's specialty. A page of questions here, a day of notes there and, if we're lucky, a handout and some pair work for a period. I just can't focus like that. Forty-five minutes straight of doing the same thing drives me up the wall. I can't even work on art for that long and art is my life."

How would you describe the teacher's feelings about the textbook? What does the student consider busy work? What types of activities does this teacher incorporate into class lessons? How do you feel about the text(s) that you use in your own teaching? Choose one lesson from the text or core book that you use in your class. Rewrite the lesson, paying attention to incorporate as many different learning/teaching styles as possible.

6. Think about a lesson that was memorable in your own schooling. Describe briefly what made it so impressive in the table on page 61. Now, take the following survey. Note how many elements listed formed part of your memorable lesson. How did each element affect the way you understood the lesson's concepts?

Think of the most effective lesson you have presented to your own students. What differences do you notice? What are the similarities? Write a brief description of both lessons, comparing and contrasting the teaching and learning styles represented in each one.

7. Look again at the cartoon at the start of this chapter. What message is the artist trying to convey? Do you feel that your teaching resembles that

My most memorable lesson ...	✔	Details
Presented material using auditory stimuli		
Presented material using visual stimuli		
Was interdisciplinary		
Included many cultures		
Involved parents/community		
Incorporated the arts		
Involved guest speakers		
Included hands-on activities		
Incorporated technology		
Involved students in critical thinking		
Made use of "authentic" materials		
Provided students with examples of multiple viewpoints		
Used materials from a variety of sources		
Encouraged creativity and exploration		
Involved reflection and encouraged action		

teacher's? What do you think your students would say? Show the cartoon to several of your students. Ask them to describe what they see. As they respond, listen for references to specific teaching styles. Do they mention their own teachers? Do they make reference to their own learning styles? Now draw two cartoons: one representing yourself as the teacher, and one representing yourself as a student. How are these two images different?

Cultural Exploration

1. *Explore other schools:* Make a "virtual field visit" to the Gardner School (*http://www.gardnerschool.org/*). This independent school in Washington state uses Gardner's multiple intelligences research as the framework for much of its curriculum. Under the "About Gardner" tab, explore the mission statement, curriculum description, and multiple intelligences list. In what ways is Gardner's theory woven throughout the school's curriculum? Create a mission statement for your classroom that takes into account your students' learning styles and/or multiple intelligences.

2. *Explore your school:* Spend a day making visits to an art class, a music class, a physical education class, a foreign language class, and an English class. Which teaching styles predominate in each class? For each class, write a list of the activities you observe. Analyze your observations. What styles are being used in each class? Which styles are not? Design a lesson for your own class that incorporates some teaching styles that you have not used in the past.

3. *Explore literature:* Read the picturebook *Yolonda's Genius* by Carol Fenner, in which a young girl recognizes her brother's musical intelligence. Interview a student who you have noticed has a particular special talent. Ask the following questions:
   - Who noticed your talent first?
   - When did you realize that you had this talent?
   - What do you do to nurture this talent?
   - Does this talent help you in school? If so, how? If not, why not?
   - How does having this talent make you feel?

 Internet Connection

Learning Styles (LD Pride)

A good beginning site, with explanations about learning styles and multiple intelligences. It also includes interactive learning style and multiple intelligences tests and strategies for success in the classroom.
http://www.ldpride.net/learningstyles.MI.htm

Howard Gardner's "Project Zero"

Information about multiple intelligences and how the theory has been applied in schools. Click on "Research Projects," then on "Multiple Intelligences Projects" for descriptions of recent studies.
http://pzweb.harvard.edu

Multiple Intelligences for Literacy

Aimed at working with adult literacy education, this site contains teaching suggestions, references, and resources.
http://literacyworks.org/mi/

Institute for Learning Styles Research

Of particular interest on this website are the description of seven perceptual styles and the list of dissertation abstracts and related research. A Perceptual Modality Preference Survey helps the visitors determine which senses they most use in learning.
http://www.learningstyles.org/

References and Recommended Reading

Armstrong, T. (1994). *Multiple intelligences in the classroom.* Alexandria, VA: Association for Supervision and Curriculum Development.

Bruner, J. (1986). *Actual minds, possible worlds.* Cambridge, MA: Harvard University Press.

Bruner, J. (1990). *Acts of meaning.* Cambridge, MA: Harvard University Press.

Campbell, L., & Campbell, B. (1999). *Multiple intelligences and student achievement: Success stories from six schools.* Alexandria, VA: Association for Supervision and Curriculum Development.

Collins, K. (2003). *Ability profiling and school failure: One child's struggle to be seen as competent.* Mahwah, NJ: Lawrence Erlbaum Associates.

Dewey, J. (1938). *Experience and education.* New York: Collier Macmillan.

Gardner, H. (1983). *Frames of mind: The theory of multiple intelligences.* New York: Harper Collins.

Gardner, H. (1989). *To open minds: Chinese clues to the dilemma of contemporary education.* New York: Basic Books.

Gardner, H. (1991). *The unschooled mind: How children think and how schools should teach.* New York: Harper Collins.

Gardner, H. (1999). *Intelligence reframed: Multiple intelligences for the 21st century.* New York: Basic Books.

Kiefer, B. Z., (1995). *The potential of picturebooks: From visual literacy to aesthetic understanding.* Upper Saddle River, NJ: Merrill/Prentice Hall.

Kolb, D. A. (1984). *Experiential learning: Experience as the source of learning and development.* Upper Saddle River, NJ: Merrill/Prentice Hall.

Levine, M. (2003). *A mind at a time.* New York: Simon & Schuster.

Mamchur, C. (1996). *A teacher's guide to cognitive type theory & learning style.* Alexandria, VA: Association for Supervision and Curriculum Development.

Sarasin, L. C. (1998). *Learning style perspectives: Impact in the classroom.* Madison. WI: Atwood.

Silver, H. F., Strong, R. W., & Perini, M. J. (2000). *So each may team: Integrating learning styles and multiple intelligences.* Alexandria, VA: Association for Supervision and Curriculum Development.

Tomlinson, C. A. (1999). *The differentiated classroom: Responding to the needs of all learners.* Alexandria, VA: Association for Supervision and Curriculum Development.

Socioeconomic Status

A Place to Begin

The 2000 United States Census defines the three dimensions of socioeconomic status (SES) as income, occupation, and education. Thus, your finances, job, and schooling define your status, your place on the scale.

The issue of socioeconomics in schools is a complicated one. On the one hand, in the United States we mandate schooling for all students regardless of SES. On the other hand, we know that schools in wealthier areas have access to better materials, better-qualified teachers, and generally more funding than do schools in poorer areas. While no two schools can be termed "equal," this disparity leads one to question whether the education that students receive in different schools is equitable.

Due to these socioeconomic differences, some states offer parents the opportunity to send their students to a school other than the one in the district where they live. This idea of "school choice" allows parents in typically low-SES areas to send their children to a school with better resources. In most states, this choice is granted via a lottery system and is seen by many as a "ticket" out of a failing school. The change in schools may also mean a change in neighborhood for the child. Along with the neighborhood shift can come a change in dominant language, culture, ethnicity, and race of the student body into which the child is moved.

While many schools are homogenous in that most students are members of the same or similar SES group, there are also many schools in which the SES levels of the student body are mildly to wildly diverse. The signals that reveal a student's socioeconomic status are many and varied. The most obvious sign is appearance, specifically one's dress. Schoolage children tend to be very fashion conscious and are keen observers of what everyone—including their teachers—is wearing. In many cases, students are accepted by their peers only when wearing the "in" brands of jeans or sneakers, or carrying a trendy book bag. A child wearing shabby clothing in school is frequently labeled as a misfit or an outcast.

Family finances come into play on other occasions in school, as well. These include outside field trips, fundraisers, and sales, and at the other end of the continuum free lunch programs. Students asked to pay for trips to museums, movies, or other venues are often put in the position of having to either ask for assistance or decline to participate in the activity. Many schools set up scholarships just for this purpose in an effort to mitigate the costs of travel for underprivileged students. Similarly, fundraisers and sales can highlight, sometimes embarrassingly, students' social and economic levels. Events that on the surface seem innocuous, such as Mother's Day plant sales, holiday gift bazaars, and participation in trade book clubs, can force a poverty-stricken student to confront the issue of money in the school setting.

The cartoon at the start of this chapter depicts two water fountains. The white one, labeled "rich," is bigger, and higher off the ground than the black one, labeled "poor." This is a reference to a time when both drinking fountains and schools were segregated in this country. The artist forces the viewer to confront the relationship between race and socioeconomic status. What connections might we make between the cartoon's portrayal of the White House and possible school issues regarding race and socioeconomic status?

NARRATIVE 8

Before You Read

Think about the occasions for which students are encouraged to bring money to school. Do you have sales events—plant sales, holiday gift boutiques, or book clubs—in your school? For what purpose(s) is the money being raised? Are school field trips organized that require students to pay for some or all of the day's activities? How often during the year are students asked to bring money? For what reasons? Do you have any support systems in place for those students who are unable to bring money for these events?

The Book Sale

I became very disappointed in one of my students one day, however, in some ways, I think the school is partially to blame. I am a student teacher in a public elementary school located in a wealthy neighborhood. The parents of many of the children who attend this school fund much of the abundant classroom materials and numerous school functions that the children enjoy. Some of the resources come from individual parent donations while the rest come from parent-led fundraisers such as book fairs, auctions, and bake sales. It seems as if the wealthier parents (primarily the mothers) of this community throw a fundraising event almost every week. While these events do generate money for the school, they also take a up a lot of class time since the teachers are expected to bring their classes to them at scheduled times.

We were scheduled to go to the book fair fundraiser with our students. While I know that these kinds of benefits yield a great deal of money for the school, I cannot help feeling uncomfortable about the whole situation. The mother-volunteers seem to use this time to wear their jeans and "get dirty" while they gossip about the new principal or fret about the middle school application process. The socioeconomic disparity among the students is blatant and, for the most part, ignored. Some students show up with 50 dollars to spend, while others have little or nothing. There seem to be unspoken rules to this game that each child (and parent) knows well. Students with no money to spend are relegated to sitting at the lunch tables while the children with money skip from book table to book table with dollars clenched in their hands trying to decide what to buy. Some collect an armful of books and wind up with a pile on the ground to choose from, while others seem to peruse each book and scrutinize the cover before they decide to hold onto it. All the while, the students without money watch, almost salivating over the books that they cannot buy.

To divert their attention from the other children, I taught the children at the lunch table the game of "20 Questions." They liked the game and began to play it on their own. By this time, my cooperating teacher was ready to bring the students back up to the classroom. I was left behind to hurry along five dawdling young shoppers.

I called the students over to the long line to the cash register set up on the ice cream box and told them that they needed to make their decisions and get ready to pay. Three of them were trying to figure out how many books they could buy with the money that they had left over. Two still had 50-dollar bills crinkled in their hands, even though they had a bag of books already purchased. We ended up playing a money game to figure it out how much they would need to buy the books they had in their hands. The two girls with the 50-dollar bills went first and we quickly determined that they had enough. Two of the other's had just enough to purchase three small paperback books and each had to put a 20-dollar Britney Spear's diary back on the shelf. While the two girls returned the diaries, I turned to the remaining girl, Ivy, and asked her if she had enough money for the three books that she held. We played the money game and Ivy realized that she needed three more dollars to buy that last book. The two other children waiting on line also computed that Ivy did not have enough money for all three books. To them, it seemed like more of a math game, just matter of fact, as if I was posing a math problem at the board and they had solved it. For Ivy, however, this discovery seemed much more than a simple game. Her face fell and she turned the three books over in her hands. She inspected each of the covers, front and back. She looked over at the girls juggling stacks of books in their arms and paused, almost expressionless. We were already late for class, so I told her to return one of the books since she could only afford two of them. She pushed up her glasses and just stared up at me incredulously. At that moment, I was not sure what she wanted me to do. It seemed as if she wanted me to recant my statement.

One of the other girls suggested that she put away *Poppleton Has Fun* since she believed that it was not as good as *Pinky and Rex and the School Play* or *Young Cam Jansen and the Lost Tooth*. This sparked a lively debate among the other children waiting on line. Ivy did not seem interested in their discussion. Instead, she continued to look down at her three books and wait. The line started to move and Ivy took a few steps ahead to keep her spot. I knelt down next to her and told her that she had to go back to the book tables and put one of them back because we were about to approach the cash register. After a long, exasperated sigh and a rolling of her eyes, she finally went to the tables to put away one of the books.

I started helping the remaining children with their money while they balanced their piles of books. Ivy returned back in line behind me. By this time, we were the last ones left and I wanted to hurry the children up so that we could get back to the classroom. Little did I know, but I was about to get a quick lesson myself.

I turned to Ivy and noticed that she still had all three books. I asked her why she did not put one of the books back, and again told her that she did not have enough money for all three. She put one hand on her hip and told me in a factual manner that one time she was with her dad at the deli and they were only charged 7 dollars for sandwiches when it should have been 9, so they got 2 dollars free. She informed me that she was going to see if the same thing would happen today. By the matter-of-fact expression on her face, I understood that she did not see this attempt as unusual. Could it be that, since she had seen it happen before, she wanted to see if it could happen again? Perhaps in her mind, "getting away with it" was just a part of the deal—something that happened if she was lucky.

I told her that that would not be fair to the school—that the proceeds of the book sale were meant to benefit the school, and that cheating knowingly would be stealing. She looked over her glasses at me, said that she was going to try it any-way, and pulled the books closer to her chest. At this point, I expected a battle to ensue and envisioned myself tearing at the extra book in her hand. My trepidation in-creased when I noticed that the four other children had overheard this conversation. Ivy did not seem to notice them, she continued to look ahead and stare at the cashier. I knelt down and obstructed her line of vision so that I would have eye con-tact and informed her that I would not tolerate stealing in my school and that she needed to chose a book now or have none at all.

Her resolute expression did not change as she laid all three books in front of the cash register. Instead of taking one of the books away myself, I chose to inform the cashier that this child had enough money to buy only two of the books and that she was having a hard time choosing which one to put back. The cashier told Ivy that she was about to close up for the day and that she had to make a decision. The child seemed incensed that I would give up her scam. She stomped one foot on the ground and glared up at me. After a brief hesitation, she picked up the top book and tossed it to the side. The cashier picked it up and said, "Someone is not having a very good day today." Ivy rolled her eyes and waited for her change. The other girls silently ob-served this scene but said nothing to either Ivy or me as we walked silently up the stairs back to the room.

Aside from being annoyed that Ivy would blatantly defy me, I felt saddened that she might think that it was acceptable to steal. How many of these kids think that they could have done the same thing? Is this something of another generation (I don't remember kids thinking this way when I was a child)? Perhaps most of these children were never given money to spend on their own in the first place. I learned that a child can be taught some pretty powerful lessons about "real life" and the rules of the game from their parents and from experiences beyond school. As a teacher who only sees these children for five hours a day, I am forced to question how much can I really change them. Is my ideal of a classroom community naïve? The classroom environment is supposed to be one where all children are given an equal shot. This ideal becomes impossible when they need to bring money. The disparities between the students are already apparent, they don't need this evidence of family financial inequity thrust in their faces. That morning's lesson taught me a great deal about the challenges I will have to face as a teacher in creating the community I would love to work with.

Questions to Consider

1. Have you ever been in a similar situation, in the student's place? In the teacher's place? How did you feel?
2. The girl explained that she and her dad were mistakenly charged less than they should have been at at the deli. Would it be appropriate for you to respond in any way to the girl's statement? If so, what would you say?
3. How would you explain to the girl why you were upset with her actions?
4. The author questions, "Is this something of another generation (I don't remember kids thinking this way when I was a child)?" What do you think? Is the situation in the narrative a generational one?
5. Should functions/trips/events where the children bring/use their own money be allowed in a public school? Why or why not?
6. What type of lesson could you create for your students that would focus on the issue of socioeconomic differences?

NARRATIVE 9

Before You Read

Think about your and your students' socioeconomic status. Are they similar or different? If different, how? Does this difference affect the way you teach your students? If so, in what ways that you are aware of?

If someone were to visit your classroom without knowing anything about your school, would the visitor be able to guess at your students' SES? At yours? How might this be possible?

What are the teaching materials like in your classroom? Do any of the objects in your room have a special meaning in a different culture? How can you find out?

Good Intentions

"And what do you want to be when you grow up?" This is the famous question that plagues children throughout their formative years. For me, the answer was simple. I always wanted to be a teacher. From the day I entered kindergarten, teaching became a life goal.

I was raised to respect everyone, whether different from or similar to me. I was taught to give each person a fair shake unless they give you valid reasons to change your mind. I grew up an enthusiastic individual, creative and giving. When Albuquerque, New Mexico, started its first kindergarten program, it called to me.

Moving is always an experience. Transplanting myself from the northeast to the southwest was an experience and a half. New Mexico's cultural diversity, climatic variations, and geographic singularities were all eye-opening differences compared to my Brooklyn way of life. I found that it actually took about two years to "de-citify." I kept comparing everyone and everything to my New York reference points. In fact, I actually had the audacity to think that because they responded more slowly, many of the people I encountered were just not up to par, intellectually speaking, with New Yorkers in general. Imagine the ego! In reality, I finally realized, just because I spoke and responded more quickly than most people I met did not mean I was superior in any way. It actually showed that I was foolishly rushing through things that wiser adults had learned to take more slowly. Reactions to time vary throughout cultures, and they have nothing to do with intelligence.

Fortunately, I had the opportunity to live in New Mexico a few years before I officially became a teacher there. I can't imagine how many more mistakes I might have made otherwise. Still, when I was offered that first teaching position, all misgivings flew from my mind as I eagerly contemplated the challenges of the trilingual program I was to work in. That first day, as parents dropped off each shy, frightened, curious, defiant, or sullen child, the challenges began:

"Remember, respect your teacher, and don't get into trouble."

"Enjoy yourself."

"Tell the teacher you can read."

"Don't let anyone make fun of the holes in your shoe."

Each set of parents left their children with different messages, different priorities.

Almost any teacher's first year is memorable. For some, the memories are positive. For others, including me, painful mistakes **are** only lightened by future accomplishments and an essential sense of humor. I meant so well, after all. High praise from my professors and happy student teaching experiences, a great new class environment with the newest supplies and equipment—what could go wrong? Three decades later, I laugh at that question.

Five-year-olds tend to be egocentric in their drawings and make themselves or a particular important object larger than life. One child had drawn his experiences growing up on a Navajo reservation and had created a picture with appropriate scale—a small child, with big mountains and sky. I loved it! I beamed about the work to the class, holding the child's picture up for all to see. However, that innocent praise was interpreted as fostering competition, a taboo concept in the Navajo culture, the culture of that child and of most of the children in the class. It was only the first day, and some students had already been alienated and lost respect for their teacher. Quite a start. I meant well, though.

Using didactic materials in different ways and seeing their possibilities is practically a requirement for any effective teacher. Kindergarten equipment and activities particularly encourage creative alternatives. For example, the children had fun working in groups with the water table, a big, recessed table placed in the classroom for hands-on activities. After a few months, though, we got bored with the water and a second medium seemed necessary.

I thought to myself: "I'm in New Mexico. What is easy to obtain, cheap, and great for measuring, weighing, and sculpting? Pinto beans!"

So, off I went to the store to buy the beans. I filled that table with one hundred pounds of beans, and the water table was transformed. We would use the beans for counting, for crafts, and for sorting activities. It was wonderful—or so I thought.

After a new activity center was in the classroom for a while, it would then become required. Each day included specific independent and teacher-directed activities. The pinto bean table became an independent activity, complete with directions to follow and specific tasks to accomplish. I planned to assign five children to it every day, until this cycle was finished. The first day, I recall one of the girls complaining that Rafael wasn't doing his work. Since she frequently tattled on her peers, I didn't give it much thought. As there was no written paperwork as a followup and I was busy with a teacher-directed activity, the incident quickly left my mind.

The second day, I noticed two boys fooling around with each other, instead of working at the pinto bean table. This was definitely surprising, since almost everyone had fought for the opportunity to work at the water table. I left my activity to quickly speak to them, but did not really have the time to pursue it. Still, I did notice that the boys were not accomplishing their required tasks and seemed to spend most of their time talking together. During nap time one of the boys was restless, which gave me the opportunity for some quiet conversation. When I asked him why he didn't do his activity work he wouldn't look me in the eye. He mumbled a bit about not feeling like it, and then said he wanted to nap. I was shocked. This particular student never wanted to nap, and grabbed every opportunity imaginable to talk with me. Something was going on, but I was clueless.

On the third day, there was again some disruption at the bean table. One girl began crying and went to sit by the hamster cage. I went to investigate, but all she would tell me was that Roberto was making fun of her. Neither child would give me details. Parents are an invaluable educational asset, and a volunteer worked in my room every morning. On this particular day, the volunteer was a mother who had spent a great deal of time with me coordinating kindergarten projects. We were comfortable with each other, and had discussed many different topics throughout the term. At the end of the day, she asked to speak with me in private. I noticed her staring at the pinto bean table. I had learned not to rush conversations, and so I waited while she composed her thoughts. She told me that I was a wonderful teacher, and that her son was learning a great deal in school. She looked at the table, and then at me and said, in a soft voice, that those pinto beans could feed her family for a year. Rafael and his friends didn't want to work at the bean table—it would mean playing with, and thus disrespecting, their food. Roberto was teasing his classmate about how she wished she could take the beans home for her mother to cook. After my parent volunteer left, I remember wanting to leave the room too, but my feet wouldn't work. I felt numb. The next day I replaced the beans with sand.

I learned a lot that first year, and a good teacher's education never really ends. I still find myself telling students to look at me when I'm talking to them, even though I know that some cultures teach their children just the opposite as a means of showing respect to adults. I still publicly praise and chastise students at times for myriad reasons, even though I'm sometimes a bit surprised at what's coming out of my mouth. After three decades in the profession, I've finally made peace with my shortcomings as well as my strengths. But one lesson persists—good intentions, respect, and consistent fairness are all important in the quest toward becoming a quality educator, but they're just ideals until put into sensitive, appropriate action. With the best intentions, we can still get important things wrong. We must ask questions of our students, our parents, and our community to discover what is important and valued in their cultures. The intention to do so is just not enough.

Questions to Consider

1. The narrator compares the speech style in the southwest to that of the northeast (i.e., her impression of speakers with a slow, southwestern accent was that they were somehow intellectually inferior to those who speak faster). How do you react to different accents? Do you place value on one or another style of speech?

2. How can teachers learn about their students' cultural backgrounds? Considering time demands, what is actually feasible?

3. What can a teacher do to correct a cultural *faux pas?* Would it have been best to apologize to the specific students and parent about the beans? Should the teacher discuss the issue in class?

4. Is public praise and punishment appropriate? If so, at what times? If not, why not?

5. How can teachers develop relationships that enable open discussion between family members and educators while maintaining a necessary, professional distance?

Project and Extension Activities

1. Look at this graphic depiction of Maslow's (1970) Hierarchy of Needs:

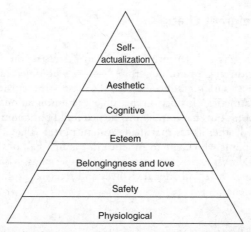

Source: Wikipedia, *http://en.wikipedia.org/wiki/Imag:Maslowsneeds.png.*
Reproduced by permission under the GNU Free Documentation License, Version 1.2.

Which of these needs intersects with socioeconomic status? How might low SES affect each level of the pyramid? In what ways? At which level do we expect kids to function at school? What needs must be met before a student can meet our expectations? Make a chart, using each need as a column heading. Under each heading, write a list of things that you as the classroom teacher can do to meet that need.

2. Read these letters from the *Queens Tribune*,* a local newspaper in Queens, New York, known as the "most ethnically diverse place on the planet." (Please note: the *Queens Tribune* publishes letters reflecting all viewpoints. The thoughts expressed in these letters do not reflect the viewpoint of the newspaper. Personal names have been suppressed to preserve the writers' anonymity.)

Letter 1: Stop the Immigrants

To The Editor:

The "concerned citizen" from Flushing (who recently wrote to the *Tribune*) is right.

Foreigners resent us Americans in *our* country. They get subsidized housing, food stamps, Medicaid, plus an SSI check that they did not work for, all at our expense, and think they are better than we are.

The other voice,———, (who recently wrote to the *Tribune*) is right too. They all come to take from *us*. Why do they all land here in Queens? We, the people, don't want them, and they don't get the message.

If they were anything in their own country, they would not come here. We have to put up with [it] because of politicians, who, I am sure, don't live with them.

A Concerned Citizen, Jackson Heights
Issue: October 19–25, 2000

Letter 2: Immigrant Check

To The Editor:

Three letters . . . recently appeared in Letters to the Editor (*Tribune,* Oct. 12), criticizing a prior one from ———, who objected to our opening the floodgates to immigration. Apparently, these three females are not too familiar with American history on the subject of immigration.

They point out that immigrants helped build our country by hard work and provided other assets that made America great. They failed to identify these immigrants who came to America in the first half of the 20th century and arrived almost exclusively from Europe—Germans, Irish, Poles, Italians, etc. They came here to better their lives and received no financial aid from the government.

*Reprinted by permission of Tribco, LLC.

The "Johnny-come-lately" immigrants came after World War II and were primarily from Central and South America, Mexico, India, the Orient, the Islands south of Florida, etc. They came here mostly to "freeload" from the "gravy train" set up by our ineffective politicians—Welfare, Medicaid, food stamps, etc. despite the fact that they have contributed nothing into the programs.

I recently read that the population of New York City is 55 percent immigrants and growing in that direction. In the near future, the immigrants will run the city and eventually the nation. I'm sure they won't be as generous to the native Americans as we were to them.

I propose we grant all immigrants a reasonable time to apply for citizenship and if they fail to do so, deport them.

————, **Forest Hills**
Issue: October 27–November 2, 2000

Letter 3: Time to Stop Immigration

To The Editor:

————'s letter in the *Tribune*'s Oct. 5–11 edition "No More Immigrants" generated controversy, for and against.

Those who want people to come to the U.S. wrote that nearly all people in the U.S. are immigrants or descendants of immigrants.

This is true. However, conditions about 150 years ago and more were entirely different from today. Then the U.S. was largely undeveloped so the immigrants came, cleared the land, built homes, stores, factories, office buildings and created farms, etc.

When the legal and illegal immigrants come to the U.S. today, they will want homes, jobs, send their children to school. This means that certain areas can become more congested, jobs can go to these immigrants instead of citizens, and schools can become even more overcrowded.

If immigrants go on welfare, this means more taxes to the citizens. It is time to stop immigration. Let the people go to other countries.

————
Issue: November 23–29, 2000

What are some of the writers' main complaints about immigrants? Outline the debate regarding this "new" wave of immigrants versus waves in the earlier part of the twentieth century. What types of economic supports are mentioned? Write your own letter in response to any of those reprinted here.

3. Look again at the cartoon at the start of this chapter. What message is the artist trying to convey? What do the water fountains symbolize? In what ways is the artist connecting race and socioeconomic status? Create a cartoon that represents your impression of the importance of socioeconomic status in your school.

4. Look at these statistics:

2004 College-Bound Seniors Test Scores: ACT
Approximately 1.17 million test takers

Family Income	Composite Score
Less than $18,000/year	18.0
$18,000–$24,000/year	18.7
$24,000–$30,000/year	19.4
$30,000–$36,000/year	19.9
$36,000–$42,000/year	20.4
$42,000–$50,000/year	20.9
$50,000–$60,000/year	21.3
$60,000–$80,000/year	21.9
$80,000–$100,000/year	22.5
More than $100,000/year	23.5
No Response	21.1

Source: ACT Inc., *ACT Assessment Results 2004.* Reprinted by permission.

Do the statistics imply anything about the ACT exam? If so, what? Write an editorial about the impact of family income on high-stakes test scores.

5. Read these quotes:

a. From *The Little Prince,* Antoine de Saint-Exupéry, 1943 (pp. 9–10):

"I have serious reason to believe that the planet from which the little prince came is the asteroid known as B-612.

"This asteroid has only once been seen through the telescope. That was by a Turkish astronomer, in 1909.

"On making his discovery, the astronomer had presented it to the International Astronomical Congress, in a great demonstration. But he was in Turkish costume, and so nobody would believe what he said.

"Grown-ups are like that. . . .

"Fortunately, however, for the reputation of Asteroid B-612, a Turkish dictator made a law that his subjects, under pain of death, should change to European costume. So, in 1920 the astronomer gave his presentation all over again, dressed with impressive style and elegance. And this time everybody believed his report."

b. From *Obedience to Authority,* Stanley Milgram, 1974 (p. 16):

"The role of the experimenter was played by a thirty-one-year-old high school teacher of biology. Throughout the experiment, his manner was impassive and his appearance somewhat stern. He was dressed in a gray technician's coat."

In Milgram's revolutionary study of obedience, subjects were asked to administer electric shocks to a subject (the shocks were fake, though the subject thought they were real). The setting and appearance of the "experimenter" were important in adding to the authenticity of the experiment, and to the authority of the experimenter.

What do these two quotes say about the importance of dress and its relevance to authority and social status?

How do your students feel about the clothes that they wear? To find out, take a survey on your students' opinions of instituting a dress code in your school. Have them elaborate on their answers and explain how and why the clothes they wear are important to them.

6. In most schools, there are a variety of events during the school year that require students to bring money to school—a school dance, a holiday bazaar, a book club, a field trip, and so on. Think about your own school context and make a list of those times when students are asked to pay for something extra. Using the list, investigate what supports (if any) are in place for students who are unable to pay for the events. In cases where supports are not available, write a proposal to your school's administration that suggests a scholarship or other fund so that all students regardless of SES are able to participate.

7. Read about the National School Lunch Program on the Food and Nutrition Service Website: *http://www.fns.usda.gov/cnd/Lunch/AboutLunch/NSLPFactSheet.htm*

Now, research the number of students in your school who receive reduced-cost or free lunches and calculate the percentage of these students in the total population (a state-by-state fact sheet can also be downloaded at *http://www.frac.org/html/news/Press_Release_04.21a.04.html*).

Interview two students, one who does not receive free lunch and one who does. How does each one feel about the program? Write a narrative that describes each student's perceptions about the program and what it means for students.

Cultural Exploration

1. *Explore people:* Interview a member of a different SES group (higher or lower) from your own. Address the following questions in your interview:
   - What, if any, visible signs reveal your SES?
   - Did/Does your socioeconomic status affect your social interactions in school? If so, how?
   - Did/Does your SES affect your academic performance? If so, in what ways?
   - Was/Is there ever a time when you were/are keenly aware of your SES in a school situation? What happened? How did/do you feel?
   - Did/Does your SES affect your choices in life? In what ways?

Using the answers to these and other questions from your interview, write a brief biography of the person. Share it with your interviewee and ask for feedback as to its accuracy.

2. *Explore other schools:* Visit one school in your area that is considered high SES, one that is middle, and one that is low. Use this comparison chart to list elements you observe for each school:

	High SES	Middle SES	Low SES
Physical plant (i.e., walls, desks, rooms)			
Curriculum (i.e., basic, enriched)			
Students (i.e., race, ethnicity, attendance rates)			
Materials (i.e., supplies, books)			
Activities (i.e., sports, clubs, trips)			

Write a brief report comparing and contrasting what you observed for each of the three schools.

3. *Explore literature:* Choose to read about socioeconomic or class issues.

Novels, Short Stories, Memoirs: choose one

- *Amazing Grace,* Johnathan Kozol
- *Rachel and Her Children,* Johnathan Kozol
- *A Hope in the Unseen,* Ron Suskind
- *Nickel and Dimed: On (Not) Getting by in America,* Barbara Ehrenreich
- *Star Teachers of Children in Poverty,* Martin Haberman
- *Unequal Childhoods: Class, Race, and Family Life,* Annette Lareau
- *Dividing Classes: How the Middle Class Negotiates and Justifies School Advantage,* Ellen Brantlinger
- *Growing up Poor: A Literary Anthology,* Robert Coles, Randy Testa, & Michael Coles, Eds.

Young Adult Literature: choose two

- *More Than a Label: Why What You Wear or Who You're With Doesn't Define Who You Are,* Aisha Muharrar
- *The Circuit: Stories from the Life of a Migrant Child,* Francisco Jiminez
- *Fast Talk on a Slow Track,* Rita Williams-Garcia

- *Esperanza Rising*, Pamela Munoz Ryan
- *No Place to Be: Voices of Homeless Children*, Judith Berck

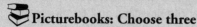**Picturebooks: Choose three**

- *If the Shoe Fits*, Gary Soto
- *Friends from the Other Side*, Gloria Anzaldua
- *A Castle on Viola Street*, DyAnne DiSalvo
- *The Hundred Dresses*, Eleanor Estes
- *The Rag Coat*, Lauren Mills
- *Changing Places: A Kid's View of Shelter Living*, Margie Chalofsky, Glen Finland, Judy Wallace, & Ingrid Klass (Illustrator)
- *Lives Turned Upside Down: Homeless Children in Their Own Words and Photographs*, Jim Hubbard

Write a reaction to the literature you have chosen. Address the following questions:
- What were your thoughts about the class issues in your chosen literature before reading?
- Did those thoughts change after your reading? If so, how?
- Did you learn anything new about the issues? What, if anything, surprised you?

 Internet Connection

The National Association for the Education of Homeless Children and Youth

A list of state coordinators is provided as well as some informative fact sheets in PDF format. You can join the NAEHCY listserv or research current legislation and policy regarding the education of homeless youth.
www.naehcy.org

The National Coalition for the Homeless

Presents facts about homelessness and a collection of personal stories from both youth and adults. There is an excellent collection of K–12 curricular resources in PDF format on the site divided into preschool, elementary, middle, and high school lessons and materials.
www.nationalhomeless.org

Poverty and Race Research Action Council

Click on the "Poverty/Welfare" link for a list of articles, advocacy updates, available grants, and other resources, including a hyperlinked list of recent articles and other information regarding poverty, homelessness, and employment.
http://www.prrac.org/

Welfare and Poverty Research

From the homepage, click on the "Welfare and Poverty" link on the right side of the page for a list of projects being conducted. For information on welfare and poverty, click on "Projects and Research" on the left side of the page and scroll down to "Fact Sheets."
http://www.childtrends.org

Equality and Education

A Century Foundation project, this site proposes socioeconomic integration of schools. Click on the "Classroom Inequality" link for articles on topics such as finances, teachers, discipline, curriculum and standards, home inequality, and summer schooling.
http://www.equaleducation.org

References and Recommended Reading

American Federation of Teachers. (1999). *Lost futures: The problem of child labor: A teacher's guide.* Washington, DC: Author.

Anyon, J. (1995). Race, social class, and educational reform in an inner-city school. *TC Record, 97*(1), 69–94.

Books, S. (2004). *Poverty and schooling in the U.S.: Contexts and consequences.* Mahwah, NJ: Lawrence Erlbaum Associates.

de Saint-Exupéry, A. (1943). *The little prince.* New York: Harcourt. English translation © 2000 by Richard Howard.

Duncan, G., & Brooks-Gunn, J. (Eds.) (1997). *Consequences of growing up poor.* New York: Russell Sage Foundation.

Fennimore, B. S. (1994). Addressing prejudiced statements: A four-step method that works! *Childhood Education, 70*(4), 202–204.

Halpern, R. (1988). Parent support and education for low-income families: Historical and current perspectives. *Children and Youth Services Review, 10,* 283–303.

Kahlenberg, R. D. (2003). *All together now: Creating middle-class schools through public school choice.* Washington, DC: Century Foundation.

Knapp, M. (1995). *Teaching for meaning in high poverty classrooms.* New York: Teachers College Press.

Kozol, J. (1992). *Savage inequalities: Children in America's schools.* New York: Perennial.

Kozol, J. (1995). *Amazing grace: The lives of children and the conscience of a nation.* New York: Crown.

Kugler, E. G. (2002). *Debunking the middle class myth: Why diverse schools are good for all kids.* Lanham, MD: Scarecrow.

Maslow, A. (1970). *Motivation and personality,* 2nd ed. New York: Harper & Row.

Milgram, S. (1974). *Obedience to authority.* New York: Harper & Row.

Persell, C. H., & Cookson, P. W., Jr. (1985). Chartering and bartering: Elite education and social reproduction. *Social Problems, 33*(2), 114–129.

Rothstein, R. (2004). *Class and schools: Using social, economic, and educational reform to close the black-white achievement gap.* Washington, DC: Economic Policy Institute.

Rose, M. (1993). *Possible lives: The promise of public education in America.* New York: Penguin.

Shapiro, T. (2001). *Great divides: Readings in social inequality in the United States.* Mountain View, CA: Mayfield.

Sizer, T. R. (1992). *Horace's school: Redesigning the American high school.* New York: Houghton Mifflin.

Spring, J. (2003). *Educating the consumer-citizen: A history of the marriage of schools, advertising, and media.* Mahwah, NJ: Lawrence Erlbaum Associates.

Sexual Orientation

CHAPTER 6

Copyright © Daryl Cagle, Cagle Cartoons, Inc. Reprinted by permission.

A Place to Begin

Chances are good that you have taught, or are now teaching, gay kids. Whether you are an elementary teacher or you work with college students, you are interacting with people who self-identify as gay, lesbian, bisexual, transgender, or questioning. To help you understand and serve this population effectively, it may be helpful to start with some definitions:

- LGBTQ: an acronym for Lesbian, Gay, Bisexual, Transgender, and Questioning
- Lesbian: a woman who is attracted to other women
- Gay: a man who is attracted to other men; also, a general term for homosexual people
- Bisexual: someone who is attracted to people of both sexes
- Transgender: someone who identifies with the opposite gender (i.e., if born a male, identifies with being a female)
- Questioning: someone who is undecided about their sexual orientation

Although in your school you may have had discussions, workshops, or staff development on many topics related to multiculturalism, far fewer teachers are exposed to research on the topic of LGBTQ youth. As we can see in the opening cartoon, prejudice against homosexuals and homosexuality is still viewed as acceptable in many realms of society. In schools, it is one of the issues that is still frequently ignored.

Consider again the ubiquitous family tree assignment and how it may affect students with gay family members:

> Throughout my childhood and adolescence, incidents like the family tree assignment left me feeling very lonely and very freakish. I vowed (to myself) to never tell anyone that my mother was a lesbian and I tried as hard as I could to never invite friends to my house in fear that they would question our living arrangements. When friends did come over, and if they asked, I would lie and say that the spare bedroom was my mother's room. Lying about my home life like this was extremely stressful and depressing. I felt certain that no one else lived like me. In my heart I didn't feel that my mother's relationship with her partner was wrong but I did feel resentful at times, especially in my teens, because we seemed so different from all of the other families that I knew. Teenagers spend most of their time striving to fit in, and life at home with my two moms did not make this easy. The shame and secrecy were heavy and to make matters worse and even more complicated my siblings seemed to have their own vows of silence, so we never even spoke about it among ourselves. It was there looming over us, but throughout our teen years we felt more comfortable avoiding the obvious. It wasn't until I was in college that I spoke of it with anyone at all. It was then that I realized that others had gone through the same thing as myself and I finally began to feel free. Most importantly, my pride was able to rise to the surface and I could proclaim all of the wonderful things about my family.

This student could not share her "untraditional" family tree with her classmates or teacher for fear of revealing a part of her identity that she felt would not be accepted in the school setting. She opted, instead, for silence rather than open herself up to criticism, ridicule, or harassment.

But not all prejudice against gays and their families ends in name-calling or verbal abuse. Read this short narrative about a hate crime from the *Safe Schools Newsletter* (Reilly, 2001, n.p.):

> At the beginning of the school year in 1999, a sophomore at a South Shore High School began a series of progressively offensive acts of harassment and intimidation against a fellow classmate whom he believed to be gay. For example, the harasser allegedly would flip his hands up and down at his wrists while saying the victim's name with a flamboyant tone of voice, call the victim a "homo" or a "fag" while glaring at him, and repeatedly tell him "Nobody likes you." Fearful of retaliation, the victim did not report the taunts to the school administration. Six months of alleged harassment and intimidation culminated in a vicious attack on the victim in the crowded school cafeteria. The assault, in full public view of other students and teachers, demonstrated that the harasser was not deterred by the potential of being disciplined by school officials, nor was he concerned about other students witnessing the assault. As a result of the assault, the victim suffered extensive bruises, internal bleeding and a punctured eardrum. After the attack, the victim purposely arrived late to class because he was afraid of having to endure further harassment. The harasser is no longer attending the school.

While not all harassment ends in such extreme violence or in a hate crime, the epithets and more subtle prejudice that LGBTQ youth suffer also have serious effects in terms of self-esteem, connectedness, and overall quality of life for these young people. Consider the following statistics from the Gay, Lesbian and Straight Education Network (GLSEN) (Kosciw, 2004):

- 81.8% of youth reported hearing homophobic remarks such as "faggot" or "That's so gay" frequently from other students. (p. 6)
- 18.8% of students reported hearing homophobic comments made by school staff. (p. 6)
- 75.1% of youth who reported feeling unsafe at school claimed that these feelings were due to either their sexual orientation or how they express their gender. (p. 12)
- 30.6% of youth missed at least one class and 28.6% missed a whole day of school in a period of a month due to feeling unsafe in school. (p. 13)
- 23.9% of youth reported frequent verbal harassment in school. (p. 14)
- 22.4% of youth reported sometimes, often or frequently suffering physical harassment (being pushed, shoved, etc.) in school due to their sexual orientation. (p. 14)
- 16.9% of youth reported some incident of physical assault (being punched, kicked, injured with a weapon) in the past year due to their sexual orientation. (p. 14)
- 57.9% of youth reported that they had personal property damaged or stolen in the past school year. (pp. 16–17)

These alarming statistics underscore the dire need for talk on the issue of sexual orientation as it relates to the identity of young children in the educational setting. Why is this topic still such a hard one to deal with in schools?

Before You Read

Think about holiday celebrations in your school. Which holidays does your school celebrate? How does the school leadership decide which holidays to celebrate and which ones to ignore? What happens to students and teachers who are not able to participate in a particular celebration?

Consider the following description of the legal status of LBGT couples (G. Bynum, personal communication, Fall, 2004):

> Lesbian, gay, bisexual, and transgender people in the United States are currently struggling for their legal rights. In 1986, the Supreme Court decision *Bowers v. Hardwicke* upheld the right of states to enforce sodomy laws that criminalize non-heterosexual sexuality. U.S. sodomy laws have been used in courts legally to justify the following rights violations: (1) prosecuting people for engaging in consensual, adult, non-heterosexual sex, (2) causing non-heterosexual people to lose their jobs because of their sexuality; and (3) removing small children from their mothers just because the mothers were lesbian. However, in a step forward for human rights, the Supreme Court overturned *Bowers v. Hardwicke* with the 2003 *Lawrence v. Texas* decision, which made all U.S. sodomy laws illegal.
>
> Lesbian and gay marriages are still prohibited in most states in the U.S. Recently at the federal level, in the U.S. Congress, there have been two important events in the struggle for legalized gay marriage. They are the 1996 passage of the Defense of Marriage Act (DOMA); and the failed 2004 effort to pass the Federal Marriage Amendment. DOMA did the following: (1) legally established that, if one state legalizes gay marriage, other states will not have to acknowledge non-heterosexual marriages performed in that state; and (2) established that, in federal legislation, marriage is defined as a union between a man and a woman. The Federal Marriage Amendment was proposed because some members of Congress were afraid that DOMA might be overturned by a court ruling. If it had passed, it would have prohibited gay marriage more strongly by adding to the U.S. Constitution a definition of marriage as being only a union between a man and a woman.
>
> Article 16 of the Universal Declaration of Human Rights states that all people "have the right to marry and to found a family," and that the family "is entitled to protection by society and the State." Although it opens with the statement that "men and women . . . have the right to marry," suggesting the idea of heterosexual marriage, it does not specifically restrict marriage to heterosexual couples.

Now consider the families that are part of your school community. What is considered a "traditional" family structure in your community? What is considered "alternative?" How are families included in your school's curriculum?

Instead

By the first Monday in May, Mother's Day advertisements hung everywhere. There were two-for-one car wash specials, super-slashed prices on men's clothing; even prescription drugs competed for a share of the Mother's Day market. Whatever the day meant to mothers, to the rest of the town it was a valuable commodity.

Late that afternoon, I played back a cheery voice message from Ms. Mandy, our daughter's elementary school teacher. "See, the problem is, Mother's Day is part of the school curriculum," she explained. "So, uh, how . . . how would you like us to handle it?" I wasn't sure if it referred to the Mother's Day curriculum, our daughter in relation to it, or the rest of the class in relation to our daughter. But I supposed that, bottom line, the teacher was referring to my spouse and me: the Gay Fathers of Room 212. "Is there someone," she inquired, "that Sarah could give the finished project to, instead?"

"Aw, no," Marcus winced, sweeping into the kitchen to throw down two bags of groceries and his keys. "Tell me I didn't just hear that." The plastic bags crashed onto the counter, sending one of them onto its side. Big, red hearts ran through their centers with "Happy Mothers Day!" stamped across them, the apostrophe in Mother's omitted. "You heard that," I said and kissed him hello.

"End—of—messages," announced the speakerphone flatly. "Again with 'instead'?" Marcus complained, saying the word not nearly as sweetly as Ms. Mandy had spoken it. He dropped his suit jacket beside the fallen bag that was sweating now from the frozen goods inside. "Press—one—to save . . ." offered the answering machine, which always had the same old options for dealing with a message. But to handle this call we needed new ones. And none yet existed.

"I've been too polite," I muttered, unpacking the things. "I've asked that something be done, asked—ridiculous!—when there is no question about this." Marcus hit Replay, nudged the volume on the speakerphone and, pulling me over, hugged me, whispering, "We tried; change is slow, especially in a school, you know that. We'll do more." He brushed back my hair with his palm and kissed my forehead. "Where's Sarah?"

"On a playdate," I said, "down the hall. Shh, I want to hear." Ms. Mandy's message played again like a happy pop song repeating its heartbreak chorus.

"She's certainly chipper, considering," Marcus said.

"Scared," I said. We listened for messages within the message sent by this popular classroom teacher, and felt desperate to protect our daughter from having to go through yet another weeks-long mechanical exercise just because the teacher said so, who said so just because the principal said so, who said so just because that was the way the school had always done things. I tossed the empty grocery bags into the trash. "Look," Marcus chuckled, pointing to the countertop. Like a tattoo gone wrong, Happy Mothers read backwards in red ink where the bag had lain. "That's us," he smirked.

"Don't even kid," I said. He hit Save and went to retrieve our child. I wiped down the counter.

Ms. Mandy's call wasn't entirely surprising; we were, after all, the New Minority Family on the block of the twenty-first century. Or at least that was how we heard we were perceived at Sarah's predominantly white K–12 school, if not by the nation; our two-father-family status put us on a shortlist of tokens. From the beginning, the message sent from administration was, We want you here and want you to feel equally treated. Even on the application, our first contact with the school, instead of "Mother" and "Father" under the blanks, both lines were labeled "Parent." It seemed to say "We're open, we're aware," which made for a great honeymoon on being accepted. Predictably, the honeymoon ended after September and the hard work began, bridging different cultural and political perspectives and histories. The teacher's call, like others that had come in previous years, was a call to attention. We didn't call back that day; we needed to think.

Back in October we had met with Ms. Mandy and the principal to encourage them to relax the requirements of this unit. For Sarah, as for some others, Mother's Day activities were irrelevant and yet followed her expectantly from year to year. Ms. Mandy, twenty four and in her second year of teaching, was everything that loving parents and their kids could hope for in a grade school teacher: earnest, eager, and a recent graduate of a renowned teaching college. But no training program could confer experience on its graduates, nor teach them how to fight the institutional fatigue and prejudice of others. These two things were precisely what Ms. Mandy needed in order to help us.

"What would you like us to consider?" asked the principal.

"Choice," I answered. "We're not saying, 'Don't include Mother's Day anywhere.' The time is already on your schedule; let kids who want to do Mother's Day projects do so then, rather than reading, writing, and art periods. Look, you want Sarah to give her work to someone else instead; but that should tell you the mistake you're making."

Now came this year's answer at another meeting. Only the voice changed. Ms. Mandy's tone was Professional-Friendly, but there was more. Beneath her pleasant cadence, her voice teetered, suggesting that even for her things were not as simple as they sounded. Perhaps she understood that this unit needed reconfiguring but felt powerless to change it. If she did feel that way she didn't say so, or was told not to. In any case, the intended clarity of her message was compromised by odd pauses and the repetition of certain key words that, ultimately, conveyed weird paradoxes: confident uncertainty, empathetic disconnection, discomfited relief. Relieved, that is, to put this uncomfortable matter behind her. But judging from our daughter's complicated response to the unit the year before, we simply couldn't let the matter rest.

Complicating that meeting, Ms. Mandy defended her sense of fairness and, while quoting herself talking in the classroom about different kinds of families, used the phrase, "Tell your moms and dads . . ." She stopped short, her eyes darting between Marcus and me, realizing not just the embarrassment of the moment, but that she had been leaving our daughter out of these classroom conversations for some time. "I never thought about it," she offered helpfully, "it's just what I've always said, how I grew up." I assured her that we too had grown up the same way. She recognized that placing the burden on Sarah to translate her instructions from "Mom and Dad" to "Papa and Dad," so that they made sense to her, could be distracting. "And distressing," Marcus added. Translating was a mechanical burden, but feeling left out went much deeper. Here was one problem that was immediately solvable. We suggested substitute phrases, like "Tell your families," or "Your grown-ups at home." Ms. Mandy later reported that she had easily accommodated these into her routine.

But the Mother's Day issue was harder for her. It was a "school curriculum," she and the principal had emphasized, a project administered across classrooms and grade levels. As such they felt obliged to maintain consistency. "Besides, parents would be upset if we didn't do it," both worried.

"Some parents, maybe," I replied.

What made them so uneasy? Was it having to reexamine the validity of a unit that for so long, as far as the school was concerned, seemed above question? Was Ms. Mandy's limited experience working with adopted children causing unspoken concern? Was it, though this was harder to address, about Marcus and me as a gay couple? That old, famous awkwardness with, or disapproval of, homosexuality? It was more likely some combination of these. Conflict of any sort with the school administration—especially a conflict influenced by the politics of other parents' responses—would be difficult. On the other hand, conflict seemed to come with the territory, just as it did for families like ours whose lives did not reflect key societal assumptions that informed units of study, if you called them that, such as Mother's Day. Ms. Mandy, even if she understood personally, nonetheless told us that Sarah would have to participate again.

We took a step back: Certainly other families at school were configured without a mother. Was it possible that straight single fathers received answering-machine messages like ours? One mother, we had heard, had a restraining order prohibiting her from having any contact with her boys at school; others had died tragically by illness, accident, or suicide. Grandparents were raising children whose biological parents were out of the picture completely. Such were the real and diverse family constellations at our daughter's school. In Sarah's classroom of 20 (10 boys, 10 girls), everyone else's family included a mother. Not that they always lived together. Many of the kids moved between divorced parents understood to be cordial; others skulked between venomous exes. Despite the complexity of these households, and the wide range of emotions and perspectives complicating their circumstances, the Mother's Day curriculum was assumed to be a meaningful experience—and fun.

Here were plenty of reasons beyond our own for limiting the Mother's Day, as well as the Father's Day, curriculum or for nixing them altogether. To think of any of these children having to participate in a generic Mother's Day unit was painful and absurd. Add to them the many other children experiencing a multitude of subtler parental tensions and what you had was not a personal annoyance but a community issue.

Like the unrecognized habit Ms. Mandy had discovered of saying "your mom and dad," the assumption of appropriateness seemed to spring from unexamined personal bias. To be sure, assumptions drawn from our lives are inevitable and account for a fair share of teaching decisions. But teachers who tie habitual reflection to professional thought and action are most able to separate their own past from what may be best for the children in their classrooms. The habit of reflection, at least in part, is how curricular elements such as the Mother's Day project can become more than just rote and how teachable moments that parents hear so much about can be captured to make a powerful difference. Since issues related to gay living are relatively new to the classroom, any teacher unfamiliar with or ambivalent about its wide range of behaviors and outlooks is likely to convey that uncertainty or discomfort. These teachers may fail to respond helpfully to children's questions or, worse, ignore mean-spirited name-calling, or even worse, hear it but believe it to be relatively harmless. Even though it was free of conscious malice, bias was at the heart of our school's outdated Mother's Day unit.

Ms. Mandy placed her mayday call to us because the "school curriculum" needed fixing to work in her classroom, yet her hope was to change us, as if we were the problem. Why, we wondered, had she not called the principal instead? Together with the faculty, they might have reshaped the whole unit. Why not have changed the date and renamed it "Parents' Day" or "Family Day," escaping altogether the trappings of commerce that Mother's Day had become? Curriculum isn't made of stone, after all. Isn't it closer to modeling clay, meant to move into the corners of the individual lives it shapes? If 1 child in 20 has two fathers, think what the 19 other children stand to learn by recognizing another culture and making cooperative, inclusive changes.

But Ms. Mandy's phone call expressed an expectation: it was up to us to accommodate to the curriculum, not for the curriculum to accommodate our daughter's classroom. The curriculum, her message said, was made of stone.

We took another step back: Maybe the assumption was that by celebrating Mother's Day the school would foster a link between school life and home life, the ideal Dewian accomplishment. But like most canned curricula, the read-alouds, heart-counting math, and card-and-box project for Mom had probably been invented for a particular group of children for whom it had made sense. The danger of any curricular success, then, was to mistake it as something separate from the children out of whom it had come, to believe that if it worked well for them it would work well for everyone. That explained how a Mother's-Day-for-All had gone from an unobjectionable curriculum to something harmful to some in just a few decades.

I daydreamed the perfect conversation. "Cancel it," I would say to Ms. Mandy. "You're celebrating a day created and financed by the flower and greeting-card industries to bolster sales. Every business imaginable piggybacks profits from our children's stereotyped heartstrings. Cancel it. It is not a real holiday."

"But, it is real," she would respond. "It's a national holiday, it's on the calendar."

"So is Easter," I would say, "and Christmas, but this school doesn't focus on them in studies because they don't represent the diversity of its students. Well, Mother's Day doesn't represent the diversity of your students, either."

"But," she would add, tiring, "you can't live in a bubble; this unit is in most people's interest, and they don't want to give it up for you."

"Martin Luther King, Jr.," I would say, inspired.

"What?"

"King fought against that argument his whole life. Whites didn't want to give up the their profitable ways to accommodate blacks. King said talking about accommodation only highlighted whites' presumption of superiority. But due consideration, equal access, and these views of power sharing, he said, would set a new course in cultural relations. What," I would say, backing up, "do you want to celebrate?"

"Mothers!" Ms. Mandy would say, frustrated.

"But you're calling us because our daughter isn't growing up with a mother. She isn't missing one. That role, in terms of parenting, does not exist. Neither Marcus nor I are substituting for a mother. We are both fathers by design, together by design, and from this framework we need schools, teachers, and fellow parents to fashion an appropriate, relevant model not just for conceiving of our family, but for re-conceiving the family itself."

Hah! Ten points! I only wish I had said that.

"I was calling," she actually did say when we spoke, "because I thought there might be someone else—an aunt or a grandmother—who Sarah could make something for, instead."

"Instead" is the message our well-meaning teacher would send our daughter. "Instead" is the message she would teach every child in her classroom by keeping the curriculum mandate, as well as the underlying social prejudice, intact.

When you're in the minority, especially the vast minority, it's never clear how much room you're permitted to take. And asking for equity when doing so calls for the majority to change, especially the vast majority, can feel to both sides like the call for fairness is itself unfair. This is a terrible irony. It was easier, I'm sad to admit, for our school to become "nut-free"—banning peanuts and all nut oils and products containing them for the well being of three students—than it has been for scores of children to be spared a subtler, emotional toxicity.

When I returned Ms. Mandy's call that first week of May, the best I could do was politely reiterate that the curriculum could be made optional or dropped.

She gave a short, friendly laugh. Suddenly, I had the distinct impression that I was talking to the school building itself: to stone, to brick and mortar dating back more than a century. "It's impossible," she answered, swift as an arrow. Then it hit me: I was speaking to something bigger than a school, beyond a curriculum. I was speaking to Mass Culture, to Historical Tradition, to Religion, to a Global Society more fixed than brick, harder than stone. As Ms. Mandy breezily pushed for the name of someone in our daughter's life for whom she could make a card and a box, I felt what I worried our daughter had felt in class: odd rather than different. I felt too unprepared, too small, somehow, to require equity. I swallowed my instinct and belief that giving in would hurt her, if only unconsciously, and teach the wrong lesson to her classmates about her family and theirs. I gave Ms. Mandy the name of Sarah's grandmother. That was all, to my own disappointment, I was able to muster.

Recently, I spoke with a teacher who told me affably that, actually, I was mothering my child. "Actually," I responded, "I'm fathering my child. I am a father, I'm fathering, but in ways you may be used to crediting to mothers." In another instance, a professor and researcher in the field of child development lectured, "And the mother during breast-feeding provides the child with skin-on-skin contact, essential for its social and emotional growth." The audience bowed their heads to write. "Nurturing an infant with touch and warmth," I spoke up cautiously, "is gender-neutral, isn't it? Fathers provide skin-on-skin contact during infancy, too, during bottle-feeding and when their infants sleep on top of them, listening to the rhythm of their hearts."

The professor bit her lip. "I suppose," she said, leafing through her notes. "It's possible but it's not in the research. But I can see how a dad might mother a child in some way."

"Father," I encouraged. "Father a child."

"Right," she said, but nobody wrote it down.

We have a long way to go. But we're going.

Gay parents like my spouse and me are guaranteed hundreds of conversations with teachers, administrators, and policy makers. But gay parents, whether single or coupled, did not invent the motherless, happy home, just as lesbian mothers did not invent the fatherless, happy home. They are new contributors to an old but un-documented story. As always, schools and their staff must listen closely to find out who their children are, who they are a part of, and how closely they can respond in support.

America—and, I suppose, the world—still believes that mothers raise the kids. Many people still assume that the act of giving birth equals the act of parenthood, and others assume that if there is no mother then it's sad and something is miss-ing. I hear this all the time because of my two-father-family status. As a nation, we don't yet have the experience of knowing the father as a nurturer. Surely, many men have been, are, and will be, but it hasn't entered our collective consciousness, not yet. A trip to any book or video store for children will quickly confirm this. There is at best one tacky book available showing gay men as loving nurturers—and they're raising a cat. The two-father family is new and offers us all another opportunity to expand the images, abilities, and responsibilities of fathers as infant nurturers and nurturers beyond.

So what do we do? As always, we meet history with history. When curriculum is treated as if as if it were made of stone, then I say we take our lead from the Egyp-tians who knew that stone, with craft and effort, could be designed and sculpted to meet the needs of society; so persistent were they that they harnessed water, stone's near opposite, to float tons of it from one city to another. We should be no less persistent in our schools and elsewhere, recasting our methods no matter how entrenched and "normal" they seem.

Let our daughter set the last example: In the end, although she had been told by her teacher that she would be making a Mother's Day card and a painted box for Grandma, Sarah surprised everyone. During the week of Mother's Day, my sister gave birth to a boy, whom we went to visit. Knowing my mother would be there, we in-vited Sarah to bring her artwork along. But that evening, holding the pinkish-bluish fingers of her infant cousin in one hand and the pinkish-bluish box she had made in the other, Sarah gently left the gift on top of the baby's blanketed feet. "Happy birthday!" she sang and turned to us, gaily squealing, "Daddy! Papa!" and leapt up into our arms to get kisses instead.

Questions to Consider

1. What alternatives do the parents suggest to the "traditional" Mother's Day celebration? Which suggestions might work in your school context? Which ones would not be accepted? Why?
2. The narrator describes the initial message from the school administration as, "We want you here and want you to feel equally treated." In what ways is this message conveyed to the parents? In what ways are these words con-tradicted by actions in the school?
3. How does changing ordinary classroom language (i.e., from "moms and dads" to "grownups at home") help to create a more inclusive classroom?

Can you think of any other such terminological changes that you can make in your own teaching?

4. The narrator is upset that the teacher called him to find out what he and his spouse "wanted to do" about their daughter celebrating Mother's Day in school. He questions why the teacher didn't contact the principal with the "problem." What might you have done in the same situation? What criticisms does the narrator make about the flexibility of the school's curriculum?

5. The narrator posits several reasons as to why the school continues to celebrate Mother's Day. List them. Are they valid reasons, in your opinion? Why or why not? How do you feel about schools celebrating Mothers Day?

6. The teacher claims that Mother's Day is a real holiday because it's "on the calendar." What does this belief imply about holidays that do not appear on the calendar? Can you think of a holiday of importance to you that is not on any calendar? How does its absence make you feel?

7. How does the teacher's suggestion to create a card for an aunt or grandmother help to maintain the status quo? What would you have suggested Sarah do?

8. The narrator makes a point of saying that he is "fathering" his child (not "mothering," as some have suggested). How do you feel about the terms mothering and fathering? What elements of gender identity are linked to each role?

NARRATIVE 11

Before You Read

We, as members of society, sanction certain behaviors as "normal" and proscribe others as "abnormal." Those who display "abnormal" behaviors are often inclined to hide themselves to avoid criticism, discrimination, and even violence.

In your school, think about students or teacher who may be hiding elements of their identities from friends and colleagues. Why do you think this coverup is necessary in each case? How do you think this act of hiding affects them? What do you think would happen if these people were to reveal their true identity to the school community?

External Faces/Internal Voices

From prekindergarten to 12th grade I attended a "liberal" school system based firmly in the ideas of diversity, ethics, and community service. After 14 years of debating ethical issues in classrooms and attending schoolwide assemblies covering everything from issues surrounding immigration in America to the ambiguities of gender and sexuality we, the students, were supposed to be intelligent and progressive thinkers. This, (in addition to creating an impressive list of college destinations), was the school's mission.

As a senior in high school it seemed that the school's mission had been fulfilled in me. I believed firmly in the equality of all people, civil rights, civil liberties, choice, freedom, privacy, diversity, democracy, and ethics. I would readily stand up against bigotry, sign petitions, walk for causes, and advocate for the freedom of speech and lifestyle. I was, by the school's definition, a "progressive" thinker.

Halfway through my senior year the content of my "progressive" character was challenged. It was not challenged by another person or idea, but by something internal, something basic within myself. I began to realize that one of my female friends and I were mutually attracted to one another.

It is rare to find a person in America who, from the moment of realizing homosexual feelings, stands tall and "out" and proud. Our culture seems to dictate that one's realization be covert, as though being "in the closet" were an essential part of the homosexual experience. I was not an exception. The realization of my homosexual feelings and the construction of my closet occurred simultaneously. Along with my closet came the ambiguity of terms and definitions. At the time I never defined myself as gay, homosexual, lesbian, or even bisexual. I called my feelings what they were without broader cultural definitions: love, infatuation, passion, or extraordinary friendship. It did not occur to me until later that both my instinctual creation of a closet and my resistance to defining my feelings as homosexual were in conflict with the values that I was taught and actualized in school. On an intellectual level I never believed that homosexuality was wrong, but when it became a reality in my own life I hid from the reality and was unable to embrace it.

It was several months before I was able to admit my feelings to my friend, who was no more secure with her feelings than I was with mine. Once we acknowledged our mutual attraction we were faced with two different but related decisions: how we were going to deal with our relationship to one another, and whether and how we were going to present our relationship to our high school community. The emotion that most colored these two decisions was fear: fear of condemnation, fear of the unknown, fear of unmovable stereotypes. We saw before us a "liberal" community and held an intellectual understanding that there was nothing inherently wrong with homosexuality. Yet, we both recoiled. What followed for the next several months was an underdeveloped relationship based on ambiguities, avoidance, and uncertainty. Our relationship manifested itself in lingering eye contact across a classroom, extra contact in a basketball game, drives around the block before class, notes in the library, legs touching in the cafeteria, and all-night phone calls. Our fear essentially created an adolescent relationship.

We were in a closet with walls several layers thick. The outermost layer contained what we hid from our community—the simple fact of a relationship beyond friendship. The next layer contained what we hid from our closest friends—the passion underlying extra glances, lingering hugs, or sudden disappearances from group activities. And the innermost layer contained what we hid from ourselves—the truth that what was happening between us was not just an experiment; that we were pursuing something that scared us so deeply we couldn't even give it a name.

However, in some ways it was this closet and the energy generated by keeping such a large secret that fueled the relationship. It was no coincidence that the relationship ended rather suddenly within a few days of our graduation. At the time I pointed to a plethora of adolescent reasons for the breakup. But in retrospect I believe that the relationship lost steam because we were losing the community we were keeping the secret from. Graduation meant that we could no longer define ourselves in relation to what our peers perceived us to be. It forced us to confront our relationship in real terms, to find words for what we were and for what we weren't. "Progressive" as we were, our relationship was unable to sustain the implications of such self-definition.

In the months after high school I grappled with many questions concerning my identity. One of the more difficult questions that I faced was the lasting effect of my lifelong liberal education. How, after all those years of ethical debates, activist speakers, and diversity panels, was I still unable to deal with the reality of my own being? How could I understand and believe in something intellectually, but be afraid of it in reality? Why was it okay for other people to be gay, but not myself? Had my liberal education failed me?

It took me several years to fully understand that there is a difference between accepting diversity in others and accepting your own identity. My school did not fail me. I had absorbed all the lessons and values that they set out to teach me—I was an open-minded, progressive-thinking member of society. But the ability to love and embrace my own sexuality was not something that my school could have targeted alone. School, family, society, and oneself must mesh together to create an all-encompassing message of self-love. When I realized that I was gay I was in a school system that was willing to embrace me, a family that rarely spoke about sexual politics, a society that still cringed at the sight of two women kissing on TV, and a self that had never before had to deal with being a minority within my community. Embracing one's own status as different from the mainstream is an uphill battle that every individual must win for themselves. There is no one-size-fits-all, blanket solution.

Now, five years later, I still fight for self-acceptance and I still struggle to match my deepest emotions with what I know intellectually to be true. I still become nervous whenever I 'come out' to a new person and I am still uncomfortable with public displays of affection with my girlfriend. The difference is that I am no longer under the illusion that hiding myself in a closet will make my sexuality easier to deal with.

I was a freshman in college when Matthew Shepard was killed in Laramie, Wyoming. The day the story was released my girlfriend came to me with a new look of fear in her eyes and said, "There are people out there who would kill us." When I am asked why in this day and age I still hesitate to come out to new people, I always think about that comment. The fact is that no matter where we live, what we are taught, who our friends and family are, there is still violence and hate out there. I do not believe in living in fear or in going into hiding to avoid the judgments of ignorant people. I believe in standing up and in coming out because, if nothing else, exposing people to homosexuality is the best way to create an accepting environment. But the death of Matthew Shepard, the overwhelming lack of antidiscrimination laws for homosexuals, and the fact that there are only two states in America where homosexual couples can have governmentally recognized unions, burns in the back of mind all the time. My schooling may have been liberal and progressive, but the world outside is wide and often prejudiced and hateful.

Questions to Consider

1. What does the narrator mean by the terms liberal (school system) and progressive (thinker)? Define these terms for yourself. Is your school considered "liberal?" are your students encouraged to be "progressive thinkers?" If so, how? If not, why not?
2. The narrator describes constructing a "closet" in which to hide her identity. What are some things that she does to cover up her feelings for her friend? Why do you think she feels the need to hide?
3. The author feels that part of what fueled her relationship with her friend was the secrecy with which they carried out their meetings and contacts. Do you think that this was the case? Why or why not?
4. Try to answer the author's question: "Why was it okay for other people to be gay, but not myself?" What role does self-hate play in this author's narrative?
5. If the narrator had come out to her friends and teachers in your school, how would people have reacted? How would you have reacted? Why?

Project and Extension Activities

1. Look at cartoon on the following page:
   Do you believe that being straight or gay is an "either/or" issue, or do you feel that there is room for a "gray area?" Where do you locate yourself on the Kinsey Scale? Survey a group of colleagues about their location on the scale. Draw the scale, placing you and your friends at the points they reported. Do the results surprise you? Why or why not?
2. Reread the description of the hate crime at the start of this chapter. Someone might have intervened at several points in this story. Does your school have a policy about harassment? If so, what is it? If not, develop a plan, using this case as a sample. What would you do at each stage of the incident?
3. What are some ways in which you might create a safe classroom/school/community? Design a proposal for your local administration or school board.
4. Read the following Federal Marriage Amendment, as proposed in the U.S. House of Representatives (H.J. 56, 2003).

   Marriage in the United States shall consist only of the union of a man and a woman. Neither this Constitution or the constitution of any State, nor state or federal law, shall be construed to require that marital status or the legal incidents thereof be conferred upon unmarried couples or groups.

Now read this abridged version of the Universal Declaration of Human Rights (United Nations, 1948):

Universal Declaration of Human Rights

Article 1 Right to Equality

Article 2 Freedom from Discrimination

Article 3 Right to Life, Liberty, Personal Security

Article 4 Freedom from Slavery

Article 5 Freedom from Torture, Degrading Treatment

Article 6 Right to Recognition as a Person before the Law

Article 7 Right to Equality before the Law

Article 8 Right to Remedy by Competent Tribunal

Article 9 Freedom from Arbitrary Arrest and Exile

Article 10 Right to Fair Public Hearing

Article 11 Right to be Considered Innocent until Proven Guilty

Article 12 Freedom from Interference with Privacy, Family, Home, and Correspondence

Article 13 Right to Free Movement in and out of the Country

Article 14 Right to Asylum in other Countries from Persecution

Article 15 Right to a Nationality and Freedom to Change It

Article 16 Right to Marriage and Family

Article 17 Right to Own Property

Article 18 Freedom of Belief and Religion

Article 19 Freedom of Opinion and Information

Article 20 Right of Peaceful Assembly and Association

Article 21 Right to Participate in Government and in Free Elections

Article 22 Right to Social Security

Article 23 Right to Desirable Work and to Join Trade Unions

Article 24 Right to Rest and Leisure

Article 25 Right to Adequate Living Standard

Article 26 Right to Education

Article 27 Right to Participate in the Cultural Life of the Community

Article 28 Right to Social Order Assuming Human Rights

Article 29 Community Duties Essential to Free and Full Development

Article 30 Freedom from State or Personal Interference in the Above Rights

Which rights are most important to you? Which ones do you believe are being violated by the proposed amendment? How do you feel about gay marriage? How do you think the issue affects children and their experience in schools?

5. Look at this cartoon:

*"If Heather has two mommies, and each of them has
two brothers, and one of those brothers has another man for a 'roommate,'
how many uncles does Heather have?"*

Think of the subject/level you teach. In what ways might LGBTQ issues be incorporated into your class? In the cartoon, the teacher has adapted a word problem in math to include a gay family. Design a lesson that includes some reference or information about LGBTQ issues.

6. Try this experiment, recording your experience and reactions in a journal: For two days do not disclose any information that reveals your sexuality. Do not mention boy- or girlfriends, dates, or the like unless you can do so in a way that hides the gender of the person about whom you are speaking. Consider these questions: Was it easy to do? What did it feel like? Did any conversations seem awkward because of this restriction? Did you avoid talking to some people? Were there times you wanted to discuss something but couldn't because doing so would reveal your sexual orientation? Try to relate your experience to that of gay students in your school who is not open with their sexuality.

7. Look again at the cartoon at the start of this chapter. What do you see occurring in the scene? Why do you think the artist chose to represent a meeting of the board of education in this way? Create a cartoon representing the way in which adults deal with the issue of sexual orientation in your school.

Cultural Exploration

1. *Explore video:* Watch the film, "It's Elementary: Talking about Gay Issues in Schools," from Women's Educational Media (*http://www.womedia.org/itselementary.htm*). Choose two of the classrooms in the film that best reflect your own school's culture. Would the lessons in the video work in your school? Why or why not?

   Design a lesson for your students about an LGBTQ, issue. Write a brief lesson plan including handouts, references, and teaching suggestions. If possible, share your lesson plan with your students, colleagues, and school leadership.

2. *Explore people:* Interview a member of the lesbian, gay, bisexual, transgender, or questioning community. Address the following questions in your interview:
   - What was/is it like to be lesbian (gay, bisexual, transgender, or questioning) in school? Were/are you "out" or closeted? Why?
   - What elements of your identity (if any) did/do you feel you had to hide in school? How did/does this make you feel?
   - Did/does your sexual orientation affect your academic performance? Your social interactions? Your relationships with your teachers? If so, in what ways?
   - Were/are you ever keenly aware of your sexual orientation in a school situation? What happened? How did you feel?
   - Did/do you ever experience prejudice or discrimination due to your sexual orientation in school? Please describe the incident(s).

   Using the answers to these and other questions from your interview, write a brief biography of the person. Share it with your interviewee and ask for feedback as to its accuracy.

3. *Explore literature:* Choose to read about lesbian, gay, bisexual, transgender, or questioning issues.

Novels, Short Stories, Memoirs: choose one

- *Out of the Ordinary: Essays on Growing Up with Gay, Lesbian, and Transgender Parents,* Noelle Howey & Ellen Samuels, Eds.

- *Am I Blue? Coming Out from the Silence*, Marion Bauer, Ed.
- *One Teacher in Ten: Gay and Lesbian Educators Tell Their Stories*, Kevin Jennings, Ed.
- *A Face in the Crowd: Expressions of Gay Life in America*, John Peterson & Martin Bedogne, Eds.
- *Is It a Choice?: Answers to 300 of the Most Frequently Asked Questions About Gays and Lesbian People*, Eric Marcus

Young Adult Literature: choose two

- *So Hard to Say*, Alex Sanchez
- *Jack*, A. M. Homes
- *Geography Club*, Brent Hartinger
- *Keeping You a Secret*, Julie Anne Peters
- *Revolutionary Voices: A Multicultural Queer Youth Anthology*, Amy Sonnie, Ed.
- *It's Perfectly Normal*, Robie H. Harris
- *Living in Secret*, Christina Salat
- *Outspoken*, Michael Thomas Ford
- *Not the Only One: Lesbian & Gay Fiction for Teens*, Tony Griman, Ed.
- *Who Framed Lorenzo Garcia?*, R. J. Hamilton
- *No Big Deal*, Ellen Jaffe McClain
- *The Journey Out*, Rachel Pollack & Cheryl Schwartz
- *Young, Gay and Proud*, Don Romesburg, Ed.
- *Hearing Us Out: Voices from the Gay and Lesbian Community*, Roger Sutton
- *Empress of the World*, Sarah Ryan
- *Free Your Mind: The Book for Gay, Lesbian, and Bisexual Youth—and Their Allies*, Ellen Bass

Picturebooks: Choose three

- *Holly's Secret*, Nancy Garden
- *The Entertainer*, Michael Willhoite
- *Daddy's Roommate*, Michael Willhoite
- *One Dad, Two Dads, Brown Dad, Blue Dads*, Jonny Valentine
- *The Daddy Machine*, Jonny Valentine
- *My Two Uncles*, Judith Vigna
- *Tiger Flowers*, Patricia Quinlan
- *Heather Has Two Mommies*, Leslea Newman & Diana Souza
- *Gloria Goes to Gay Pride*, Leslea Newman
- *Asha's Mums*, Rosamund Elwin & Michele Paulse
- *What Happened to Mr. Forster?*, Gary Bargar

Write a reaction to the literature you have chosen. Address the following questions:
- What were your thoughts about LGBTQ culture before your reading?
- Did those thoughts change after your reading? If so, how?
- Did you learn anything new about the culture? What, if anything, surprised you?

 Internet Connection

The Gay, Lesbian and Straight Education Network

An excellent resource for teachers that offers a searchable library of articles, announcements, and news clippings. There is also information about how to join the "Safe Schools Action Network" and a forum for people to tell their stories. Of particular interest is the annual report containing statistics and other research about the LGBTQ community.
http://www.glsen.org

The National Youth Advocacy Coalition

A clearinghouse of information about LGBTQ youth. This site provides links and a forum for youth to communicate with legislators on topics of importance to the LGBTQ community. Information is provided about how to establish a Gay–Straight Alliance in your school. The resource guides and database of books, videos, and other materials are also particularly helpful.
http://www.nyacyouth.org

Parents, Families, and Friends of Lesbians and Gays

An excellent resource for friends and family of LGBTQ youth that provides support and information. There are links to education (with the "Youth and Schools" page of particular interest), advocacy (news and legislative updates), and suggestions about how to set up a local PFLAG chapter.
www.pflag.org

Safer Schools

This "school survival guide" for LGBTQ youth includes an "ask the experts" section as well as a teachers' lounge with stories from teachers and students about being gay in school. Statistics about LBGTQ youth in schools are provided, as well as a listing of youth groups and community centers in every state.
http://www.centeryes.org

The Safe Schools Coalition

This site provides links to resources organized by type, topic, and "people who use them." Of particular interest are the excellent PDF handouts for students, educators, and parents such as "An Educator's Guide to Intervening in Anti-Gay Harassment." Some information is available in Spanish.
http://www.safeschoolscoalition.org/

References and Recommended Reading

Bennett, L. (1998). Teaching students to face their anti-gay prejudices. *Chronicle of Higher Education, 45*(9), A76.

Harris, M. B. (Ed.). (1997). *School experiences of gay and lesbian youth: The invisible minority.* New York: Haworth.

H.J. Res. 56, 108th Cong. (2003). Proposing an amendment to the Constitution of the United States relating to marriage. Retrieved 18 June 2005 from *http://thomas.loc.gov/cgi-bin/query/z?c108:H.J.RES.56:*

Hogan, S., & Hudson, L. (1998). *Completely queer: The gay and lesbian encyclopedia.* New York: Henry Holt.

Huegel, K. (2003). *GLBTQ: The survival guide for queer and questioning teens.* Minneapolis, MN: Free Spirit.

Kissen, R. M. (1996). *The last closet: The real lives of lesbian and gay teachers.* Portsmouth, NH: Heinemann.

Kosciw, J. (Ed.). (2004). *The 2003 national school climate survey: the school-related experiences of our nation's lesbian, gay, bisexual and transgender youth.* New York: GLSEN.

Lipkin, A. (1999). *Understanding homosexuality, changing schools: A text for teachers, counselors and administrators.* Boulder, CO: Westview.

Peyser, A. (2001, May 8). Mother's Day banned . . . *The New York Post,* p. A5.

Pinar, W. (Ed.). (1998). *Queer theory in education.* Mahwah, NJ: Lawrence Erlbaum Associates.

Reilly, T. (2001). Stemming hate in our schools. *Safe Schools Newsletter* (January), n.p. Boston: Office of the Attorney General.

Siegel, L., & Lamkin Olson, N. (2001). *Out of the closet into our hearts: Celebrating our gay/lesbian family members.* San Francisco: Leyland.

Spurlin, W. (2000). *Lesbian and gay issues in the English classroom: Positions, pedagogies, and cultural politics.* Urbana, IL: National Council on the Teaching of English.

United Nations. (1948). *Universal declaration of human rights.* General Assembly Resolution 217 A (III). Retrieved 09 June 2005 from *http://www.un.org/Overview/rights.html*

Religious Beliefs

CHAPTER 7

A Place to Begin

One major aspect of the national identity of the United States is the idea of separation of church and state. European immigrants came here in search of religious freedom, and although periodically attacked by those seeking to impose their views on the majority, this concept remains ingrained in our collective psyche. However, it is in fact practically impossible to keep one's religious identity from informing and shaping one's view of the world. A continual challenge in our nation's schools is how to implement the idea of "separation of church and state" while simultaneously not interfering with students' and faculty members' rights of free expression.

While *proselytizing* (teaching religion in an effort to convert or dissuade) is, indeed, illegal in schools, teaching *about* religion is not. However, when it comes to spiritual topics, there seems to be a fine line between teaching a subject for information and teaching in a way that would make students of a different faith uncomfortable. How, then, do we deal with religion in the classroom?

Many educators choose to completely ban religion and religious topics. Since there is such diversity of religions in the United States, it may seem impossible to teach about all of them, so many opt for teaching about none of them. However one chooses to address the issue, we as educators must, at the very least, attempt to understand our students' religious faiths and how these faiths are expressed in both overt and covert ways.

Just as many teachers assert that they are "color blind" in their classrooms, teachers often claim not to view their students as religious beings. However, religious elements can become part of the school culture as beliefs, requirements, or practices that occur during the school day. For example, although parties and celebrations are an ubiquitous part of school culture, the religious beliefs of a Jehovah's Witness preclude taking part in such celebrations. Can a teacher ignore this reality in the service of being "neutral?" Another example is that of a Sikh student. In today's uncertain climate, most districts have a "zero tolerance" policy with regard to weapons in schools. However, Every Sikh male is required to carry a *kirpan,* a small dagger that is a symbol of his spiritual commitment to justice and honor. Should this student be allowed to carry this instrument in school? There is no way to be neutral about such religious issues.

Read this short reflective piece about a Muslim teacher and her experience in school after September 11, 2001. As you read, think about what it might be like to have this woman as a student in your class.

I often wonder whether people see me as a Muslim terrorist strapped with bombs under my veil and assault rifles in my school bag. Perhaps they see me as an oppressed female whose father forced her to wear the dress of dignity. Even prior to September 11, I grew used to receiving strange looks and covert glances. Naturally, during the week of the horrific events of September 11, I was uneasy about coming to school. I feared people would lash out at me out of anger or fear, or worse, presume that because I am identifiably Muslim and Arab that I condoned the tragedy.

The day in question was off to a typical start. I was walking down the school hallway when a bunch of students glared at me as I approached and snickered as I walked by. I immediately became self-conscious and with a heightened sense of hearing, heard one student mumble, "You'll pay for this, Arab." Another student added "You and all your vile camel worshippers." I was shocked more than I was hurt and continued walking—a bit faster now.

Though I wanted to write it off as pure ignorance, I was unable to shift my thoughts elsewhere. I realized that indeed they thought that I approved of those inhumane acts. I wondered how I could possibly live with the idea that those around me deemed me to be in consent with those who murdered so many innocent Americans. It disturbed me to think that I would be exposed to such hatred in a place that I once thought so safe. I felt a powerlessness and alienation that I had never before experienced. For the first time in my life, I felt the absolute pain of being a victim of discrimination.

Those students didn't know that I am an American, that there were many Arabs and Muslims who died in the World Trade Center, and that my heart went out to those who were affected by the tragedy. When Muhammad Ali was asked how he felt about the fact that those responsible for September 11 shared the same faith he responded, "How do you feel about Hitler sharing yours?" I knew I wasn't at fault, but the constant reminder that "my people" were a threat put me on the defense.

As a result of 9/11, stereotypes against Muslims will linger longer than ever before and it's our job as teachers to educate ourselves first and then our students about different groups of people and religions. Had those students known that Islam teaches nonviolence or that the world leaders of *all* the Muslims condemned the acts of 9/11, perhaps they would have spared themselves the inhumanity of ignorance and spared me the fear I continue to live in today.

The students' comments—based only on the narrator's outward appearance that identified her as a Muslim—made this teacher feel unsafe in her own school. For teachers and students alike, prejudice based on religious identity can convert the educational arena into a place of discomfort, self-doubt, and fear.

The United States Census is prohibited by law to ask questions about religion. For this reason, it is difficult to find legitimate statistical sources about the popularity of different religions in the United States. However, according to the 2001 *American Religious Identity Survey,* Americans self-identified as the following:

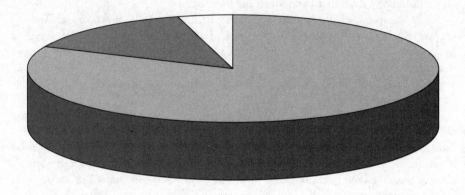

☐ 76.5% Christian

■ 13.2% Nonreligious

☐ Broken down as:

1.3% Jewish

0.5% Muslim

0.5% Buddhist

0.5% Agnostic

0.4% Atheist

0.4% Hindu

0.3% Unitarian/Universalist

0.1% Wiccan/Druid/Pagan

Source: Data are from *American Religious Identification Survey* (n.p.) by B. A. Kosmin, S. P. Lachman, and associates, 2001, New York: Graduate School of CUNY. Retrieved 21 June 2005 from *http://www.adherents.com/rel_USA.html*

While we can certainly describe a religion as "major" in a quantitative sense (i.e., a majority of Americans self-identify as Christian), this term can not be used to refer to the importance of any one religion, since this importance can only be expressed by each individual practitioner. For example, when a school claims to celebrate "all major religious holidays," who is the word *major* valid for? For a Christian, Christmas and Easter are "major" holidays. For a Muslim, Christmas and Easter are not important, but Ramadan and Id are. As in the cartoon at the start of this chapter, people are often tempted to define their own religion as important, others as less so. In the school setting, it is crucial that we give validity to and acknowledge the importance of all students' (and teachers') religions. One way to do this is to educate children about all religions while also acknowledging secular and nonreligious choices.

NARRATIVE 12

Before You Read

While we currently subscribe to the philosophy of "separation of church and state" in public schools in the United States, one's religious identity does play a role in the classroom. In what ways might your religious or nonreligious identity affect your own teaching? Is there a religious majority in your school? A religious minority? How do students of different faiths interact in your classroom? Your school district? Your community?

Within the Flock

I started my teaching career at my former high school, a parochial Methodist school with 120 years of history. Being a Catholic in a Methodist school never really bothered me much as a student or a teacher. The culture was still based on Christian principles anyway and if at all, it helped in my religious tolerance for diversity of practice within Christianity.

However, there were times as a student when I had to deal with some fellow or senior students, and some teachers, who would not confront but would "challenge" me with questions about certain arguable aspects of my faith, such as whether Catholics prayed to Mary or why we went to a priest to confess our sins. I was still going to Sunday school at my church then and I remembered sharing these questions with my Sunday school teacher in an effort to find answers. These challenges helped me clarify my understanding of my faith in Catholicism and provided me with a "weapon" for future challenges. I graduated from school a much stronger Catholic than when I first entered and did not convert, thankfully for my parents, to Methodism. I come from a very staunch Catholic family and I sometimes wonder what my parents, especially my father, would have felt if I had converted to Methodism, since he was actually responsible for choosing the school in the first place.

When I joined the school as a teacher, I recall hearing some colleagues commenting that I was "still not saved," but I decided to ignore these comments. My status as a Catholic was generally not an issue as a teacher and the more enlightened members of the school administration focused more on the fact that I was a Christian rather than on our differences in doctrines and beliefs. These differences were most apparent in my contributions to the school morning devotions, which I would conduct regularly during the school term. Devotions are daily events held in morning assembly before the whole school, and involve some form of reading from the Bible and a commentary on the teachings as applicable to the students and teachers.

When I was first approached to conduct devotions as a new member of the school teaching team, I was apprehensive. I worried that my commentary might cause some dissent or uproar, should what I say contradict the principles of

Methodist theology. I was very careful about what I wanted to say and actually wrote out a script, which I shared with the vice principal to check for contradictions. She told me it was unnecessary and waved me off. She was a Baptist herself and as vice principal conducted the devotions at least once a week. I decided that it really did not matter because there were more commonalities about any Bible passage than there are differences between Catholicism and Methodism. However, I later discovered that some teachers felt excluded from my presentations because they were being conducted by a Catholic.

I was always open about my religious background with both my colleagues and my students. Sometimes I did feel that being known as a Catholic teacher in a Methodist institution must be like being identified as gay—I felt I must be feeling the same sort of exclusion. As it turned out, though, because of my religious orientation, some of my Catholic students began to approach me to talk about their own experiences as Catholics in the school, and I became for them a supportive role model. They knew they could turn to me for advice if they experienced religious conflicts or challenges from their peers. It was also good for me to see some of my students in my own church on Sundays.

As I grew more assimilated into the school culture, I became proud of being Catholic and Christian that I began to feel that it was within my power as a teacher to be a role model for my Catholic students, and that it was my duty to keep them "within the flock." I would take it upon myself to remind them when I saw "morally" wrong actions. At one point, one of my female students confessed to me that she had started dating a Muslim boy. I had no qualms about taking the girl aside and asking her to reconsider her relationship with someone of a different religious background, especially Islam. I tried to point out to her the challenges of interfaith relationships as well as marriages. She, of course, did not want to heed my advice, being 15 years old. She was unconvinced and said to me that they were just exploring their friendship. She did not think that the relationship would end up in marriage. I was bent on pointing out that if the relationship became serious, the Christian would have to convert to Islam. I was so afraid that she would "lose her faith." After an hour of unsuccessful attempts to get her to see my point, I gave up and decided to let the girl find out for herself what I thought would be the beginning of a disastrous relationship.

I found out a few years later that the pair broke up after they left school. And although I myself ended up marrying another Catholic, I shudder whenever I recall this incident. I feel ashamed that I had become the bigot that I sought to challenge when I was a student. What if it had been me who fell in love with a non-Catholic? Wouldn't I have continued with the relationship myself?

Questions to Consider

1. What role should religion play in public schools? Private schools? Why do you feel this way?
2. Have you ever been in a situation in which you are culturally very different from the majority of your coworkers or students? How did you deal with the situation?

3. At one point in the narrative, the author states, "Sometimes I did feel that being known as a Catholic teacher in a Methodist institution must be like being identified as gay." Why do you think the author feels this way? What stereotypes does the author subconsciously subscribe to in saying this?
4. Should a teacher give romantic or other personal advice to students? Have you ever given a student advice about a relationship? How was the advice taken by the student? Did you feel satisfied with the results? Explain your answer.
5. The author asks himself, "What if it had been me who fell in love with a non-Catholic? Wouldn't I have continued with the relationship myself?" What do you think you would do in a similar situation?

NARRATIVE 13

Before You Read

Think about the religious holidays for which schools in your district are closed. Why are they closed for these holidays and not for others? Do you have colleagues in other schools for whom classes are in session on those days (or vice versa: your schools are open on a holiday for which neighboring schools close)? How do you both feel about the disparity? In your opinion, should classes be cancelled for holidays celebrated by a minority group? For the majority? Why or why not?

Playing Soccer on Yom Kippur

I was born in Boston, Massachusetts, and spent my precollege years living in Newton, a suburb of Boston. The population of the city is predominantly white. I identify myself as a white female. The Jewish community in Newton is both prominent and thriving. My family belongs to the largest Reform Jewish synagogue in Newton, and has always been active in the Jewish Community Center. As a white, Jewish girl, I rarely felt excluded in Newton.

I am aware that Judaism has been the target of much hatred and anti-Semitism. Throughout my childhood I learned about this hatred towards Jews in religious school and Hebrew school. We learned about the Holocaust from history books and movies, and even heard personal accounts and horror stories from World War II survivors. I watched the news and saw current hate crimes, such as Swastikas painted on synagogues and Jewish cemeteries destroyed by vandalism. However, during my childhood, I never experienced this type of hatred on a personal level.

I was often surrounded by other Jewish students in school, on sports teams, and in other extracurricular activities. I never felt different when I had to miss a soccer game for Hebrew school. People in my community, even if they were not Jewish, understood and accepted my religious commitment. By no means was Judaism the majority religion in Newton, but that did not seem to matter. What mattered was that people accepted and included Jewish people in the community. If Rosh Hashanah or Yom Kippur, the High Holidays, fell on a weekday, school was cancelled, as it was for Good Friday. I never had to worry that I might fall behind the rest of the class because I missed school to attend religious services. My religion helped me to feel included in my community. It was not until later in my life, when I entered college, that I realized how different I could feel because I am Jewish, and how crucial the inclusion had been for me.

I attended a small liberal arts school in New England. When I entered as a first year, the population of Jewish students was approximately 10 percent. The small percentage of Jewish students did not interfere with my decision to attend this school. I felt comfortable enough with my religion and my Jewish identity that I did not worry about the lack of Jewish students. However, in retrospect, I now realize that for the first time in my life I understood what it meant to feel excluded because of my religion. I was amazed that I actually met people who had never seen nor spoken to a Jewish person. I met people who had never heard of Rosh Hashanah or Yom Kippur. I had to explain to friends that I did not eat bread products during the holiday of Passover. I remember being shocked that I actually had to explain that other foods such as pasta, cake, and cookies also fell into "bread product" category, and were therefore not kosher for Passover. I had a difficult time finding kosher for Passover foods on campus and in local supermarkets, a problem I never faced in Newton. However, the fact that I could not buy kosher food did not upset as much as an incident that occurred in one of my extracurricular activities.

During my freshman year, I played soccer for the varsity program, the only Jewish member of a team of 22 players. As a first-year student, I was thrilled to be a part of the varsity program. I knew it would be a challenge, but I was willing to work hard. We received a copy of our schedule on the first day of practice. As I scanned the dates for our games, I realized that there was a game scheduled on Yom Kippur. I thought that it must have been a mistake that the program had scheduled a league game on Yom Kippur, the Jewish Day of Atonement, the day in which I fast to remember my sins. Never in my life had I ever had a schedule conflict with Yom Kippur. I always had school cancelled on this holiday. I could not imagine that a liberal institution that prides itself on being racially, ethnically, and religiously tolerant would not recognize this major event. Much to my amazement, I soon discovered that this was not a scheduling mistake, but at the time, as I sat in my team meeting, I did not have the courage to ask my coach how I could fix this problem.

I was forced to make a choice. I could either play in the game and not observe the holiday, or observe the holiday and therefore be forced to sit out the game. I called my parents to ask for advice, knowing that I would not get an answer to my problems. As anticipated, my parents told me that I needed to make my own decision and that they would support me in whatever I chose to do. I came to the conclusion that this was an important holiday that I was not willing to give up. I was nervous to tell my coach, because I knew that he would not understand.

I sat in his office that afternoon and tried my best to explain what the holiday represented. I was so nervous that my voice shook when I spoke. I could feel my face become hot and red as I struggled to get the words out of my mouth. I had to tell him that not only would I not be playing, but that I also had to leave early to continue the celebration of my holiday. As I spoke, he quietly sat across from me and nodded. I remember wondering what he was thinking and what he would say when I finished. He accepted my decision, but asked me to explain to my teammates why I would not play that day. I left his office that afternoon feeling worse than when I had entered. I was neither relieved nor relaxed, and I certainly did not feel reassured about my decision. I had hoped that my coach would have commended me for making this decision and maybe even talked to the athletic director about rescheduling the game, but neither happened.

Talking to my teammates was a difficult task for me. A formal team meeting was called so that I could explain the situation to them. With only one of me, and 21 of them, I was even more nervous than when I spoke with my coach. I feared that they might think that I was not committed to the team. No one had ever sat out a game for religious reasons. Most of them had never heard of the holiday, and therefore did not know its importance in my religion. Some of the girls did not understand why I would not play, and asked questions such as, "Why don't you just go to temple in the morning, and then play the game in the afternoon?" and "Will your parents really be angry if you miss temple one year?" I had to explain that it was a fasting holiday, and therefore I would not even have the strength to play. I also had to explain that I had made this decision, not my parents. Ultimately, my teammates accepted my decision. When the meeting was over, I actually did feel a sense of relief, as if a small weight had been lifted from my shoulders.

Even though my coach and teammates accepted my decision not to play, as I reflected, thoughts ran through my mind. "Why do I have to justify missing the game? Why do I have to worry that my teammates might think I was not committed? Why do I have to wonder if I will be benched for the next game because I missed the previous game? No one ever had to explain why she could not play a game on Easter Sunday or Christmas. No one had to do that, because a game would never have been scheduled on these holidays." The more I thought about it, the angrier I became. I was frustrated that I would even have to decide whether to miss a game. I was angry because I had to justify my choice. I was angry at my teammates for questioning my decision. It was then that I realized what it meant to feel excluded. I had no support from my teammates or my coach because they simply did not understand. I felt isolated by their lack of knowledge.

I became so appalled that the game had even been scheduled that I wrote a letter to the athletic director expressing my concerns. Not only did I never receive a response to my letter, but the school scheduled a game on Yom Kippur the following season. I was unsuccessful in my attempt to try to educate others on the importance of this day. I took a stand and put myself on the line, and nothing came of it. This made me feel as if I had no voice. I realized that the athletic director and the entire athletic department at this "liberal college" were not as accepting as I had once believed. This made me wonder how many other students would have to refuse to play and justify their decision and how many other letters would have to be written before others understood. I wondered, "Would anything ever change?"

As I look back on this experience, I realize that it would be difficult to honor all major holidays for the many religions that exist. However, I also realize that there is a general understanding that games are not to be scheduled on Easter or Christmas, while this is not the case for major Jewish holidays. I do, however, feel as though my choice was right for me. In retrospect, I also realized that my teammates truly did not understand my religious commitment, and that they questioned me because of this lack of knowledge. While I might not have educated the athletic director, maybe I enlightened some of my teammates.

This experience also helped me to examine my own beliefs about religious tolerance. Because of my upbringing in my Jewish community, I rarely thought about what life was like for my grandparents and parents as Jewish people in their communities. I took for granted what generations before me worked so hard to achieve. I now listen more closely to their stories of exclusion and the hatred that they experienced and I realize that to be a Jewish person was not always as easy as it has been for me.

Questions to Consider

1. Due to this narrator's high school experiences, she went to college with some unexamined expectations regarding religious diversity. Based on your reading, what are some of these expectations?
2. The author refers to Yom Kippur as a "major event" and is surprised to find that a game is scheduled on that day. What does the word *major* reveal about the author's perspective? What does the scheduling of the soccer game reveal about the coach's and the college's perspective?
3. The coach in the story requires the narrator to explain her conflict to the team. Do you agree with this requirement? Why or why not? What would you have done in the coach's position?
4. The narrator's teammates offer several suggestions to help her avoid missing the game. In what ways do these suggestions reveal the teammates' lack of understanding?
5. The narrator chose to write a letter of complaint to the athletic director. What might that letter have said? Would you have written a letter? If so, to whom? What would your letter say?

Project and Extension Activities

1. In many states in the United States, when a child is ill and in need of medical attention, prayer is considered a legal form of treatment if the guardians of the child are members of a religious group that prescribes prayer as a viable

treatment. In the following states, this is considered an "affirmative defense" (acceptable in the eyes of the law):

Alabama	Iowa	Oregon
Alaska	Kansas	Tennessee
Arkansas	Louisiana	Texas
California	Minnesota	Utah
Colorado	New Hampshire	Virginia
Delaware	New York	West Virginia
Idaho	Ohio	Wisconsin
Indiana	Oklahoma	

Source: Data are from *Religious Exemptions to Criminal Child Abuse and Neglect* (pp. 1–2) by National Center on Child Abuse and Neglect, 1996, Washington, DC: Dept. of Health and Human Services.

Ideas about appropriate health care can be quite different for people of diverse faiths. People of some faiths are exempted from required inoculations and school vaccines due to their religious beliefs. Jehovah's Witnesses, for example, do not accept blood and so cannot have blood transfusions or undergo surgery that requires replacing blood or blood products.

What are your feelings about religion and health care? Have you ever had a difference of opinion with someone regarding appropriate medical care? Discuss the issue with someone of a different faith. Create a Venn Diagram that represents the differences and similarities of practices and opinions for you both.

2. Parties are often a large part of school culture, especially in the elementary grades. However, Jehovah's Witnesses are not allowed to celebrate or participate in parties. What would you do if you had a Jehovah's Witness in your class? Write a letter to the parents of your students explaining your decision regarding parties in class.

3. Recently an atheist, the father of a young girl, sued the state of California over recitation of the phrase, "One nation, under God" in the pledge of allegiance. How do you feel about this issue? What does it mean to be atheist? To be agnostic? How do these beliefs affect one's participation in school? Write an editorial regarding the father's case, either supportive or critical. Explain your position.

4. Read this email sent to a school principal by a teacher:

The annual winter concert has just finished. Although this is only my first year teaching here, as a Jewish member of this school community, I want to share my discomfort over some parts of this assembly with you.

For many American Jews, December is the month of the year during which we are most reminded of our "minority" status in the U.S. Many of our most symbolic public spaces—everything from the White House to Wal–Mart to television— send the message that to be truly a part of America, one must celebrate the birth of Christ.

I am usually proud of the way that our school embraces the diversity of cultures, races, religions, and sexual preferences at our school. However, I felt that today's concert was often a Christmas/Christian assembly masquerading as a secular winter celebration. The specific parts that were uncomfortable for me were the lighted Christmas tree at the entrance of the auditorium, the first song asking God to bless America, and a song that repeated, "Merry Christmas, Merry Christmas." I am confident that the staff who chose to include these elements in the concert did not intend to make anyone feel excluded, but that was exactly how I felt. It was a painful shock to attend an event that I'd been looking forward to with anticipation, only to be met with so many symbols that seemed to be saying, "This is not your assembly. You don't belong here. Our school culture does not include you."

I know our school has the potential to make every school member feel included as an equal citizen. Today, however, I felt that we did not meet this standard. I realize that there might not be a single other person who left the assembly feeling as I did. Nonetheless, I wouldn't feel right leaving the building today without sharing these feelings with you.

Have you ever been in a similar position to that of the author of this letter? If so, how did you deal with your discomfort? Imagine that you are the principal of this school. Write a letter in response to the teacher.

5. Look at this timeline of some world religions (adapted by permission from Hare, 2001):

Timeline of World Religions

2000 BCE	Hinduism
1500–1350 BCE	Judaism
628–527 BCE	Zoroastrianism
599–527 BCE	Jainism
580–500 BCE	Taoism
563–483 BCE	Buddhism
551–579 BCE	Confucianism
1–33 CE	Christianity
100 CE	Shinto

570–636 CE	Islam
1469–1538 CE	Sikhism
1817–1892 CE	Baha'i

Note that the terms *BC* ("Before Christ") and *AD* (*"Anno Domini"*—the Year of the Lord) have been replaced with *BCE* ("Before the Common Era") and *CE* ("Common Era"). Why do you think that these terms were changed? What implications does using *BC* and *AD* have in teaching history in school? Do you agree with the changed terms? Why or why not? Write an editorial piece about the change.

6. Read the following description of an incident in school:

One of my students, Farukh, had put off writing his college essay until the last minute. His teachers, myself included, were putting pressure on him to turn the work in. Finally, he decided that he would write about his life growing up in an Iranian Muslim household. In describing that experience, he explained that his mother had always been a particularly strict disciplinarian and that she hit him with sticks and had even thrown him into the walls on various occasions. In the essay he described the bruises that he had incurred in vivid detail. Needless to say, I was horrified when I read this.

I was well aware of my legal obligation to report to my superiors suspected child abuse of any of my students. The law states:

"A person who, while engaged in a professional capacity or activity described in subsection (b) of this section on Federal land or in a federally operated (or contracted) facility, learns of facts that give reason to suspect that a child has suffered an incident of child abuse, shall as soon as possible make a report of the suspected abuse to the agency designated under subsection (d) of this section."

From United States Code: *Title 42—Public Health and Welfare,*
Chapter 132—Victims of Child Abuse,
Subchapter IV—Reporting Requirements,
S 13031—Child Abuse Reporting

Teachers are one of the professionals who are required by this law to report suspected abuse. In a meeting with the principal, I informed Farukh that the school would have to contact Social Services about the incidents described in his essay. In a desperate attempt to protect his family, Farukh explained that the events had occurred several years ago and that he was no longer disciplined in that way by his mother. The principal explained that while that might be the case, he was worried about possible harm that might come to Farukh's 12-year-old sister. Farukh tried to explain that no harm would come to his sister since in his culture, girls were not subjected to corporal punishment.

Social Services did finally visit Farukh in his home. The case worker spoke with Farukh's mother and interviewed his sister and ultimately determined that there was no cause for further investigation. Farukh is thankful that the whole incident is behind him and, after writing another essay, was accepted into his first-choice college.

While Farukh can now relax and enjoy his last few months in high school, the incident has caused me to rethink my own definitions of discipline, corporal punishment, and child abuse. Although I am bound by my professional duties as a teacher to report all suspected cases of child abuse of my students, I will forever question my own definitions of abuse as they relate to the context of that particular child and his family religion and culture.

Think about ways in which culture and religion might play a role in the disciplining of children. In the United States, what accommodations are made for parents or guardians of other cultures and/or religions with regard to child discipline? Take a survey of your teaching colleagues about their opinions regarding corporal punishment. Encourage your informants to make connections between their opinions and their cultural/religious background.

7. Look at the cartoon at the beginning of this chapter. What message is the artist trying to convey? Do you agree with this message? Create an image or cartoon that somehow depicts the religious makeup of your school's student body and/or your school's attitudes towards religion.

Cultural Exploration

1. *Explore neighborhoods:* Visit a neighborhood that is predominately inhabited by one religious group. If possible, go accompanied by a member of that religion. Create an annotated map about your exploration. Include the places you visited, photos or memorabilia where possible, plus brief descriptions or reactions to each site. Address the following questions:
   - What physical signs are there that indicate which religious group lives in that area?
   - How are people dressed? Is the clothing similar to or different from your own?
   - What cultural centers do you see?
   - What religious institutions are present?
   - What signs do you see that indicate how closely and in what manner the religion and culture are intertwined?

   Discuss how your visit made you feel. Use the following continua to start thinking about your interaction with the neighborhood. (Note: Use the terms as ends of a continuum rather than as dyadic opposites. It is more likely that you would feel varying degrees of both descriptors at different points in your exploration.)

Did you feel comfortable <–> uncomfortable?
Did you feel included <–> excluded?
Were you interested <–> disinterested?

2. *Explore people*: Interview a member of a religious group. Address the following questions:
   - What does it mean to you to be a member of the _____ (religious group) community?
   - Do you feel a strong affiliation with your religious group? In what ways? In what ways not?
   - Did you ever experience prejudice because of your group membership? Describe.
   - How does being a member of your group affect the way you view the world?
     Using the answers to these and other questions from your interview, write a brief biography of the person. Share it with your interviewee and ask for feedback as to its accuracy.
3. *Explore literature*: Choose to read about a religion that interests you, or one that you know little about.

Novels, Short Stories, Memoirs: choose one

- *Nice Jewish Girls,* Evelyn Beck
- *Mona in the Promised Land,* Gish Jen
- *The Jew in the Lotus,* Rodger Kamenetz
- *Bless Me, Ultima,* Rudolfo Anaya
- *Ordinary Magic,* Malcolm Bosse
- *Crossing Guadalupe Street: Growing Up Hispanic and Protestant,* David Maldonado
- *The Spirit Catches You and You Fall Down,* Anne Fadiman

Young Adult: Literature: choose two

- *Miriam's Well,* Lois Ruby
- *Make a Wish, Molly,* Barbara Cohn
- *The Hopscotch Tree,* Leda Siskind
- *Gideon's People,* Carolyn Meyer
- *Send Me Down a Miracle,* Han Nolan
- *What I Believe: Kids Talk about Faith,* Debbie Holsclaw Birdseye
- *I Believe in Water,* Lois Ruby & Marilyn Singer
- *Ordinary Miracles,* Stephanie S. Tolan

Picturebooks: Choose three

- *The Christmas Menorahs: How a Town Fought Hate,* Janice Cohn
- *Night Lights,* Barbara Diamond Goldin

- *Light the Lights,* Margaret Moorman
- *Ramadan—Islamic Holiday,* Suhaib Hamid Ghazi
- *Muslim Child: Understanding Islam Through Stories and Poems,* Rukhsana Khan
- *Lights for Gita,* Rena Krasno
- *The Swirling Hijaab,* Naima Bint Robert
- *Our Eight Nights of Hanukkah,* Michael Rosen & Dyanne DiSalvo-Ryan
- *What I Believe: A Young Person's Guide to the Religions of the World,* Alan Brown & Andrew Langley

Write a reaction to the literature you have chosen. Address the following questions:
- What were your thoughts about the religion(s) you chose before your reading?
- Did those thoughts change after your reading? If so, how?
- Did you learn anything new about the religion? What, if anything, surprised you?

 Internet Connection

Teaching About Religion in Public Schools

A site devoted to the teaching of religion in schools in support of an educational commitment to pluralism and diversity. Descriptions of a variety of worldviews are provided, including nonreligious, Buddhist, Christian, Hindu, Muslim, Jewish, Sikh, Tao, and Deist. Also included is information about the history of the Pledge of Allegiance and recent court rulings.
http://www.teachingaboutreligion.org

Anti-defamation League—Religious Freedom

Of particular interest is the page (found under "Religious Freedom" in blue link box to left), "Religious Holidays in Classrooms." On this page is a link to a downloadable PDF guide to religious displays. Good information about religious clubs in schools and an article about teaching about religion plus some activities for parents and teachers.
http://www.adl.org/religious_freedom/

American Civil Liberties Union—Religion in Schools

From the homepage, click on "Religious Liberty" to find resources about religion in schools such as a list of current press releases, action items, and legal and

legislative documents. Also appearing is information on government-funded religion, religious freedom, and religious discrimination.
http://www.aclu.org

Religion and Education Journal

"A journal of analysis and comment advancing public understanding of religion and education." View excerpts from recent articles on topics such as religion in public schools, spirituality in the teaching profession, and interfaith events.
http://fp.uni.edu/jrae/

Equal Partners in Faith

"A multi-racial national network of religious leaders and people of faith committed to equality and diversity." Click on the "Links" tab for an excellent list of denominations and communities of faith websites.
http://www.equalpartnersonline.org

References and Recommended Reading

Beversluis, J. (2000). *Sourcebook of the world's religions: An interfaith guide to religion and spirituality.* Novato, CA: New World Library.

Delfattore, J. (2004). *The fourth R: Conflicts over religion in America's public schools.* Boston: Yale University Press.

Delpit, L. (1995). *Other people's children: Cultural conflict in the classroom.* New York: New Press.

Douglass, S. L. (2002). Teaching about religion. *Educational Leadership, 60*(2), 32–36.

Fraser, J. (1999). *Between church and state: Religion and public education in a multicultural America.* New York: St. Martin's.

Hare, J. B. (2001). *Timeline: Origin of major religions.* Retrieved from *http://www.sacred-texts.com/time/origtime.htm*

Haynes, C. (1997). *Finding common ground: A First Amendment guide to religion and public education.* New York: Diane.

Kessler, R. (2000). *The soul of education: Helping students find connection, compassion, and character at school.* Alexandria. VA: Association for Supervision and Curriculum Development.

Marty, M. (2000). *Education, religion, and the common good: Advancing a distinctly American conversation about religion's role in our shared life.* San Francisco, CA: Jossey-Bass.

McPhatter, A. R., Velasquez, J., & Yang, K. Y. (Eds.). (2003). Perspectives on cultural competence [Special issue]. *Child Welfare, 76*(1).

National Center on Child Abuse and Neglect. (1996). *Religious exemptions to criminal child abuse and neglect* (Child Abuse and Neglect State Statutes, Vol. V). Washington, DC: Dept. of Health and Human Services.

Nord, W. A. (1995). *Religion and American education: Rethinking a national dilemma.* Chapel Hill, NC: University of North Carolina Press.

Palmer, P. (1993). *To know as we are known: A spirituality of education.* San Francisco, CA: Harper.

Palmer, P. (1997). *The courage to teach: Exploring the inner landscape of a teacher's life.* San Francisco, CA: Jossey-Bass.

The Skillman Foundation. (1993). *Cultural competence: The problem.* Report of the Foster Care Taskforce to the Michigan Department of Social Services. Detroit, MI: Author.

Linguistic Diversity

CHAPTER 8

A Place to Begin

Over the course of our history several individuals and groups have attempted to establish English as the official language of the United States. Among them, the "English Only" movement of the late twentieth century is perhaps the best known. According to Census records, well over 96 percent of Americans are fluent in English. Establishing English as the country's official language would eliminate many services—such as translations and official documents in several languages—for those who are not native speakers.

Some "English Only" proponents base their position on the claim that immigrants to the United States refuse to learn English, instead establishing native-language enclaves. This is a gross exaggeration. In fact, most U.S. immigrants *want* to learn English. Private language schools abound in most American cities, and colleges and universities offer special classes to help improve the language skills of nonnative speakers of English. Commercial textbooks, video and audio programs, and other learning materials also proliferate. There is no lack of will to learn English on the part of immigrants to the United States. There are, however, some cognitive constraints on second-language acquisition, especially for students in a K–12 setting.

Children who arrive in the United States with little or no English language proficiency may be placed in a number of different settings. Most schools would offer these children English as a Second Language (ESL) classes in which they would learn content in English from a teacher who specializes in working with English Language Learners (ELLs). Some children are enrolled in bilingual programs, in which they receive instruction both in English and in their home language. In recent years, bilingual education has been heavily criticized for many reasons, the chief one being the objection to spending public dollars on education in a language other than English. However, also for many reasons, bilingual education is an important option for a great number of children.

Linguist Jim Cummins describes two types of language skills (1979): basic interpersonal communicative skills (BICS), and cognitive academic language proficiency (CALP). BICS can be seen on the playground, in the hallways, and at the bus stop. Students display BICS when they chat with friends, use slang, understand jokes, and gossip. It is the language that we all would first learn if we were to move to another country—interpersonal language. Cummins states that it takes only up to two years to develop BICS. However, the language of school, the academic language of essays, compositions, term papers, tests and reports, takes a great deal more time—five to seven years—to develop. Unfortunately for ELLs, they are judged, graded and promoted on their CALP, not their BICS.

Bilingual education programs are designed both to keep students up with their content area work and develop their English skills, allowing them to learn concepts in science, math, and social studies, for example, in their native language while also providing directed English instruction. These programs are also important in that they maintain the student's home language; studies have shown that literacy in one's first language is one of the major predictors of success in one's subsequent languages (Collier & Thomas, 1989; Cummins, 1991; Koda, 1994; Nieto, 1992; Wong-Fillmore, 1991).

But issues surrounding linguistic diversity affect not only students in ESL or bilingual classes. Any student in your class who speaks another language brings with her a variety of traits that are connected to being a multilingual person. Although we normally think about language as spoken or written, we also must consider sociolinguistic issues such as gestures (which, like language, are culturally-based phenomena), proxemics (spatial relationships), and deixis (the relativity of language). For example, speakers of some languages find it offensive to use certain gestures (such as pointing); others find them perfectly appropriate. Students from certain cultures may speak at a very close distance from an interlocutor; in the United States, this proximity is usually cause for discomfort. Such *paralinguistic* cues are culturally grounded and carry important meaning. Thus, it is important to pay attention not only to students' spoken and written language, but also to their body language.

It also is important to consider diversity in dialects and communication style in the educational context. Delpit (1995) ponders the difficulties that arise when the gap between the communication styles of teacher and students is too wide. She contrasts white and black teachers and their styles of educating black students. She offers as an example the different discourse styles of both teachers in common classroom control situations. Delpit claims that black teachers are more direct and explicit in their reprimands (e.g., "I don't want to hear it. Sit down, be quiet, and finish your work, NOW!" [p. 168]). White teachers, she feels, tend to imply a request and downplay commands (e.g., "Would you like to sit down now and finish your paper?" [p. 168]). Delpit posits that black students respond more readily to the overt display of power shown by the black teacher, since this is the type of interaction they are used to at home. Freire (2003), however, might question the propagation of such power dynamics. He might see this type of interaction as the maintenance of the status quo, with oppressed taking on the role of oppressor and reenacting roles of domination and control. Furthermore, one may question Delpit's descriptions of black and white communication styles as being oversimplified at best or stereotypical at worst.

Whatever our communication and discipline styles in the classroom, there are issues that we must address with regard to the languages and cultures of our students. As teachers, we bring to school our "invisible knapsack" filled with language-based expectations and experiences that affect the way we interact with students from a variety of linguistic and cultural backgrounds.

The cartoon at the start of this chapter depicts a conversation in which one character declares that he is "proud to be Cuban again." Why do you think he feels this way? Why do you think he reacts to the new immigrant in the way that he does? How do you normally react to a person who is not fully proficient in English?

NARRATIVE 14

Before You Read

There is great diversity among speakers of any language. Whether variations are dialects, accents, or regionalisms, these subtle differences in the ways we speak a language often reveal information about our socioeconomic standing and membership in or exclusion from subcultures and the dominant culture.

For multilingual students in your school, which language do they speak at home? At school? On the playground? Do they speak with an accent? How are their home languages validated in school?

What are the major language groups in your school community? Do you have bilingual programs or ESL programs, or both? Is your school's program a *pull-out* program (where students are taken from the mainstream classroom and sent to a smaller class to get ESL instruction) or a *push-in* model (where an ESL teacher helps students in the mainstream classroom)?

My Inferior Dialect

I am an American of Cuban descent, who grew up in a bilingual home. If you believe my elementary school report cards, my Spanish went from almost fluent to barely proficient in just one school year. The effortless As that consistently punctuated Sra. Castillo's grade book from Kindergarten through fourth grade went into hiding just before the start of fifth grade, and in their place stood mostly Cs, with a few Bs and Ds thrown in for the sake of variety. I was terribly confused. How could I have gotten so stupid over one summer? How was it that I was unable to utter a single intelligible sentence in Spanish, when for years I thought I had a solid command of the language?

Sra. Castillo, my surrogate grandmother three times a week for years, had retired. She took with her my pride in my Cuban American heritage. I lost my prized teacher's-pet status when our new teacher assumed the role Sra. Castillo had managed so well. While I missed Sra. Castillo even before the start of the school year, I was excited to meet her replacement. I wanted to like this woman as soon as we walked into her room. Who wouldn't? She looked like Barbie.

Unfortunately this Barbie's sweet smile was not a permanent fixture. She was a vicious, snobbish tyrant who took my consistent dropping of the "s" sound and final syllables in Spanish as a personal affront. Everything I did and said was not only wrong, but offensive to her delicate ears. I didn't just answer questions incorrectly, I mutilated her "pure" Spanish. A "baing pa'ca" would condemn me to public ridicule about my "classless" Spanish. Raising her blond eyebrows and puckering her mouth, Sra. Martinez would inhale dramatically as she slapped the open palm of her hand on my desk to accentuate every syllable she enunciated dramatically in my face: "*Venga para aca.*" Somehow, her corrections just wouldn't sink in. But by the end of fifth grade I was internalizing her messages about how classless and inferior Cuban dialects are.

Once I tried to defend myself, explaining that my mother's whole family dropped the same sounds and syllables as I did, and they spoke only Spanish. To me, this was proof that my Spanish was legitimate. Her stinging retort took away any cultural pride I had at that age. In sweet tones meant to sound like she was educating the class about Latin history and culture, Sra. Martinez explained that Cubans do not speak proper Spanish. It was in this lecture that I found out I had more black and Indian blood than European blood, and that the Spanish I had grown up hearing was jarring, unsophisticated, and acoustically unpleasant.

At that very moment I felt my skin growing darker, my eyebrows thicker, and my butt rounder with every word. I had never felt so different from my peers, and longed to be somewhere else, with Spanish speakers of my own kind.

After this lecture I hated Sra. Castillo, the woman who should have spent less time kissing her students on our foreheads, temples, and cheeks and more time teaching us to be and speak just like beautiful Sra. Martinez. I tried to wipe off the memory of garishly-colored lipstick kisses that had long since disappeared. My respect for Sra. Castillo faded like her kisses.

I wanted to be more like Sra. Martinez, who looked like everyone else in my Spanish group: white. I wanted to look like her, speak like her, think like her, and even walk like her. Her insight into my cultural deficiencies pervaded my thoughts, and I began to notice details of my family life that shamed me. Why did Abuela curse so much? Why couldn't she just learn English, now that she lived in the United States? Why did my mother need to wax her arms and upper lip?

A scorn for my culture was born when I was in the fifth grade, and over a decade passed before I no longer emphasized that I was only half Cuban or made up stories about my mom's family emigrating from Europe just before the Revolution. I am still struggling to quiet the reflexive mantra that repeats in my head every time I read or watch a news segment on a crime: Please don't let the criminal have a Spanish last name, please don't let the criminal have a Spanish last name, please don't let the criminal have a Spanish last name . . .

And, thank God, my last name is Jones.

After many years, I finally began to reject the hold Sra. Martinez had over me. Things are substantially different now. I no longer want to be just like Sra. Martinez. I am instead terrified of turning into her. I now student teach in a fifth grade New York City public school classroom, where several students speak nonstandard English. My cooperating teacher has explained to them the difference between the way one may speak to a friend and the way one should speak to a teacher, and asked me to insist on standard English when I speak to them or correct written assignments.

I understand why it is paramount to enforce rules about not using colloquial language in school, but I also feel badly about "correcting" the English their parents speak. When do cultural sensitivity and celebrations of diversity give way to teaching how to speak and write in standard English? Am I telling them that they do not speak English well when I mark up their papers? That is preposterous and arrogant—many speak English only, and insisting that they speak it incorrectly feels worse than hearing that my Spanish is low class.

I appreciate that Cuban Spanish is not standard, and know that I would not have done well on my AP Spanish test or similar exams if it had not been for my Spanish, Argentine, and Chilean teachers in high school. Does that mitigate the damage caused by messages I got in fifth grade about how my family speaks Spanish incorrectly? I don't know. Certainly the way this information was presented to me affected the way I felt about my heritage, but I think it would have stung even if I were corrected in a sensitive way.

I recently stopped correcting my extended family when they pronounce my name as "Pow-la." My insistence on Americanizing my name was intense, and I am left with remnants of these insecurities about my identity. Am I doing the same when I cross out double negatives in my students' writing? ¿Qué sé yo?

Questions to Consider

1. When the narrator first started school, she had a positive experience despite the language difference. What contributed to her comfort in the classroom?
2. The narrator describes her new teacher as "Barbie." What do you think she means by this? Why do you think she accepts the criticisms of her new teacher, even though they hurt her feelings?
3. Why do you think that the narrator's teacher told her that "Cubans do not speak proper Spanish?" What other information did the teacher link to this discussion of Cuban Spanish? How did the narrator react to these claims? Why do you think she reacted in this way?
4. How does the narrator resolve the issue of her cultural identity? In what ways does she identify with being Cuban? With being American?
5. Why is the "standard" dialect of a language perceived as "good" and nonstandard varieties and dialects perceived as "bad?" What positive purposes does teaching and emphasizing use of the standard dialect have? When might it be both appropriate and "good" to use a local, nonstandard dialect? What benefits accrue to acquiring the ability to switch seamlessly between nonstandard and standard varieties of a culture's dominant language(s)?

NARRATIVE 15

Before You Read

How do communicate? Are you direct and to the point or do you use more subtle ways of conveying your wishes and needs? Do you express affection openly and frequently or do you hide your feelings? When you are conversing with someone, do you stand close to that person or do you maintain your distance? Would you consider your style boisterous or rather subdued? Do people you share a cultural background with also share a particular communication style?

Does your communication style change depending on context? Are you a different communicator at home? With friends? In school? Think about your favorite teachers in your own school experience. How did they talk to the class? How did you learn to communicate successfully with a class of students? Did you model your style on any one particular teacher? Consider a class you are working with now, or one in the recent past. Try to define your communication style with this group of students.

Cultural Code Switching

"What are you planning on doing once you graduate?" I heard that question from my parents and many other well-intentioned souls too many times my senior year of college. The truth was I still had no idea, but that simply wasn't something I wanted to say to parents who had just paid for four years of college and to friends who were getting five-figure signing bonuses. Then I heard about Teach for America, an organization that takes college grads and places them in under-resourced schools across the country. It seemed like a perfect opportunity: contribute to a better world by teaching and buy myself another two years to figure out what I really wanted to do.

An interview and an acceptance letter led me to Houston, Texas, where Teach for America held its five-week training session. We dabbled in teaching and in writing lesson plans and participated in lengthy discussions about race, poverty, and the urban experience. The practice was necessary and the debates illuminating, but none of it helped me to truly picture what I was stepping into. That realization came weeks later, when I first visited my assigned school, Hamilton Elementary.

As I walked into school for the first faculty meeting, three children ran up to the security guard opening the door and begged to use the phone. They said that there had been a gang fight and people were hurt. As the security guard ushered them inside, she pointed me towards the stairs and motioned for me to go down to the basement. I found the cafeteria after only a few minutes of wandering. I sat in the back, thinking that it would be easier to hide my nerves and ignorance there. The rest of the staff began trickling in and taking their seats. It didn't take me long to realize that no amount of seat jockeying would help me to hide.

Thanks to my white skin I stuck out like a sore thumb. Only two other staff members in the room were white, the other 50 or so were black. The talks at training about working in a minority-dominated school came back to me. Finally I began to see the reality of my situation. I, a white woman from the suburbs of Ohio, would be teaching in an all-black school. Ignorantly, I dismissed the significance of my revelation, telling myself that color didn't matter in the classroom; the only thing that counted was how good a teacher I was.

This mantra repeated itself on a constant loop inside my head during the start of school. It became even louder the moment when I picked up my class of fourth graders on the first day of school and saw that all 25 of them were black. I played it again when I butchered their names during attendance. I replayed it when, in a hallway fight between sixth graders, a piece of weave was ripped off a girl's head, and I had no idea what it was. And I turned the volume up as loud as it would go when I constantly had problems in my classroom, problems that appeared to have no end.

Students did not listen to me; fights broke out; defiance was the order of the day for some of my kids; homework was nonexistent for half of them; and walking anywhere in the hallway was a nightmare. After a few months of this, I was desperate. In an attempt to determine why this was happening to me, I began looking at other teachers and trying to see the difference between us. What made them able to relate with and to manage their students? Why wasn't I able to do it? I listened in on other teachers and their conversations with their students. I snuck into the back of classrooms and scoped out their management techniques. I read book after book that promised to reveal the secret to a problem-free classroom. And still, the problems persisted.

One day, after a particularly long back and forth between myself and Gloria, a girl who refused to follow even my most basic requests, I sat alone in my classroom and once again tried to figure out why I couldn't handle my own students. Idly, I watched the students and teachers pass my classroom door, and then it hit me. All of the teachers I admired were black, and all of their students were black, too. Sure, it seems obvious, but the fact that race could enter into my classroom management problems had never occurred to me; I had been too busy telling myself that only my teaching and dedication mattered.

Now that the idea was in my head, I began to look for differences between the way that the black teachers communicated with their black students and the way that I, the white teacher, did. I noticed a few things immediately. I made requests of the students, like, "Could you sit down please?" while the black teachers stated what they wanted the students to do. I spoke unclearly and ironically to my students, saying things such as "Wow! It's loud in here!" or "Don't you think we could get to Art faster if people stopped talking?" The black teachers explicitly told the students what was expected of them. I never told my students how much I cared for them because I thought it was implied by my hard work and long hours; the black teachers touched, hugged, and showed their affection to their students with endearments like "baby" and "honey." When I got upset with the students, I yelled shrilly and confronted students around their peers; the black teachers would lower their voices and speak firmly in a no-nonsense way. They would also use what I called "parent talk." They said things like, "Boy, you better sit in that seat" and "Didn't I tell you to stop that?" I never spoke that informally to my students, thinking that I lacked the credentials to do so since I was neither a parent nor black.

As I noticed these differences, I began to toy with the idea that I could change my teaching style and communicate more the way the black teachers talked with their students. I couldn't imitate their skin color or their experiences, but I might be able to copy their communication styles. Gradually, I adopted a kind of code switching in which I was able to use the approaches of the black teachers despite my whiteness. My classroom slowly became calmer and more orderly. My students opened up more, and I began to visit their homes. We had finally reached a place where we could coexist peacefully and productively in the classroom and communicate more effectively. Teachers and the vice principal began to compliment me on the changes in my class. It seemed that my cultural code switching had paid off.

Questions to Consider

1. To what does the narrator attribute her discipline problems in the classroom? Do you agree with her assessment of the situation? Why or why not?

2. Once the teacher begins to understand the issues in her classroom, how does she go about finding answers or solutions to her problems? What would you do to try to find answers?

3. Describe the main differences in the communication styles of the white teacher and her black teaching colleagues. Have you ever noticed these or other differences in styles? If so, give some other examples.

4. Have you ever code switched? If so, in what context? Why did you feel the need to change your mode of communication at that time? Did you feel comfortable changing your style? Why or why not?

5. At the end of the narrative, this teacher states that her "code switching had paid off." Do you feel that her choice to change her communication style was a good one? Why or why not? Would you do the same in her situation? Explain your answer.

Project and Extension Activities

1. Look at these statistics:

Ten Most Common Language Groups of Limited English Proficient (LEP) Students (District LEP Services Questionnaire)

Language	Number of LEP Students	Percentage of LEP Students
Spanish	2,963,256	76.9%
Vietnamese	90,659	2.4
Hmong	68,892	1.8
Korean	47,427	1.2
Arabic	44,681	1.2
Haitian Creole	43,137	1.1
Cantonese	36,942	1.0
Tagalog	35,495	0.9
Russian	33,860	0.9
Navajo	33,622	0.9
Others	454,570	11.8
Total	3,852,540	100.0%

The number of respondents who provided data on this item was 932. The item response represented 97.8% of the weighted cases on this form. The responses were weighted at the item level to be nationally representative.

Source: From *Descriptive Study of Services to LEP Students and LEP Students with Disabilities, Volume 1A: Research Report—Text* (Contract No. ED-CO-0089) (p. 19), by A. M. Zeller, H. L. Fleischman, P. J. Hopstock, T. G. Stephenson, M. L. Pendzick, and S. Sapru, 2003, Washington, DC: U.S. Department of Education, Office of English Language Acquisition, Language Enhancement, and Academic Achievement for Limited English Proficient Students (OLEA).

Which (if any) of these languages are spoken in your community? How does your school community reflect these languages/cultures? One way to acknowledge language in a school is to post signs in that language. If you do not already have signs reflective of the community languages in your school, create them with the help of your students or language-speaking community. You can also find common words and phrases (i.e., *Hello, Welcome, Thank you,* etc.) in hundreds of different languages on the following website: *http://www.elite.net/~runner/jennifers/*.

2. Ask a colleague or student to give you a lesson in another language. Encourage your teacher to use the immersion approach in which the medium of instruction is the target language (i.e., a Gujarati lesson is taught completely in Gujarati). After your class, respond to the following questions:
   - How comfortable were you during the lesson?
   - What percentage of the time did you not understand what was going on? How did this make you feel?
   - What techniques, if any, did the teacher use to try to help you understand the lesson?

3. Propose a "Heritage Language Day" to your school administration. Encourage students, teachers, and parents to offer classes in their home languages. Create an invitation inviting other schools and community members to participate.

4. Do you speak Standard American English (SAE)? SAE is the term given to a generic form of English used mainly by TV news reporters and the like. Most everyone in the United States speaks a regional form or dialect of English, such as Black English, New York or New England dialects, the various Southern regional dialects, and so on. Write a short script or dialogue using both a dialect you know and Standard American English.

5. Read this poem about living in two languages:

At that age
I spoke but with
One tongue

Created by lullabies
Curiosity, poetry and
Song

I began to impersonate
Imitate and recreate
All that was said
And spoken

From nonexistent
To broken
Sentences grew

And took form
Speaking became
The norm

Out of the blue
I was transported
From something great
To something new

De español al inglés
I realized how
Little I actually
Knew

All the while
Feeling misplaced like a
Grown child
Taken back to infancy
Confused
Into a new world
Imposed on me

Language reintroduced
Itself as a mystery
During the time I
Had grown all I had known
Was one side
Of a coin
In a jar of thousands

Inglés was difficult
Inglés made no sense
Inglés did not care
Inglés was what others
Used to speak of me
Inglés was written on every door

Inglés spoke of love
But did not show *amor.*

While learning *inglés*
People had yellow hair
Because in my adjective deprived mind
Blonde was nonexistent.

I could not find
The path to clarity
Only disparity

And in the midst
Of frustration
From sentence
Structure, definitions
And grammatical
Complications
English spoke
Gingerly and softly
In my ear.
English revealed
A secret which
Would take me
Years to comprehend
And suddenly
I became unchained . . .
No longer *palabras*
But words were
What I learned
And retained
No longer neglected
By English with
Each word I
Felt connection
And warmth of roots: French,
Greek and Latin
As these roots of
Language esconced
Me in satin
Of knowledge divine
As two tongues in love
Became intertwined in my mind.

How would you describe the author's transition from being a monolingual Spanish speaker to being bilingual? What do you think he means by the lines, "I could not find/The path to clarity/Only disparity?"

Do you ever feel like you live in more than one culture? Write a poem about your own experiences with more than one language or culture.

6. Answer these questions (Ada, 1997):
   • Do parents have the right to be able to communicate with their children in their own language?
   • Do children have a right to preserve the language in which their parents and relatives can transmit family history, cultural values, and world view?

- Are there ethical (and legal) implications when a school district allows (facilitates, promotes) the loss of the students' home language when that home language is also an academic subject that could offer the opportunities of advanced placement, contribute to enhance entrance possibilities to college, and better employment opportunities?

  Interview several colleagues using these questions. Do the answers surprise you? Write a short report for your school about bilingual education.

7. Look at this cartoon:

Copyright © 1995, 1999 by Larry Feign. Reprinted by permission.

Do you know any students who are multilingual? Interview at least one and find out how they learned their languages and about their feelings regarding being bilingual.

8. Look at the cartoon at the start of this chapter. What message is the artist trying to convey? Create a cartoon that illustrates any experience you have had interacting with speakers of another language.

Cultural Exploration

1. *Explore neighborhoods:* Visit a neighborhood that is predominantly inhabited by a single linguistic group. If possible, go accompanied by someone who speaks that language and is a member of that cultural group. Create an annotated map about your exploration. Include the places you visited, photos or memorabilia where possible, plus brief descriptions or reactions to each site. Address the following questions:
   - What physical indications tell you which linguistic group lives in that area?
   - What linguistic cues (in verbal speech) do you hear? How did you communicate with the community on your visit?
   - What cultural centers do you see?
   - What languages are shop signs printed in. Street signs? Newspapers? What other print examples do you find?

- What type of music do you hear? What languages are people singing in?
- How do people gather (e.g., in small groups, pairs, alone)?

 How did you find the experience? Did you have any trouble communicating? What techniques, supports, and strategies did you use to ensure mutual understanding?

2. *Explore people:* Are any languages other than English spoken in your own family? Interview a member of your family who speaks (or spoke at one time) another language. Address the following questions:
- How did you learn English?
- How long did it take you to learn?
- How do you feel when you are speaking in your first language(s)? How do you feel when you speak English? Do you prefer one or the other? Why?
- Are there any incidents in the past that you can recall when you had difficulty with regard to language? Could you tell me that story?

 Using answers to these (and other) questions, write a linguistic biography of this person. Share it with your interviewee and ask for feedback as to its accuracy.

3. *Explore literature:* Choose to read about a language group that interests you, or one that you know little about.

Novels, Short Stories, Memoirs: choose one

- *Hunger of Memory: The Education of Richard Rodriguez,* Richard Rodriguez
- *Heading South, Looking North: A Bilingual Journey,* Ariel Dorfman
- *On Borrowed Words: A Memoir of Language,* Ilan Stavans
- *How the Garcia Girls Lost Their Accents,* Julia Alvarez
- *When I Was Puerto Rican,* Esmeralda Santiago
- *Growing up Bilingual: Puerto Rican Children in New York,* Ana Celia Zentella
- *Lost in Translation: A Life in a New Language,* Eva Hoffman
- *Dreaming in Cuban,* Christina Garcia
- *Native Speaker,* Chang-Rae Lee

Young Adult Literature: choose two

- *I Love Saturdays y Domingos,* Alma Flor Ada
- *My Name is Maria Isabel,* Alma Flor Ada
- *The House on Mango Street,* Sandra Cisneros
- *Say Hola, Sarah,* Patricia Reilly Giff
- *Cool Salsa,* Lori Carlson

Picturebooks: Choose three

- *Speak English for Us, Marisol!,* Karen English
- *I Speak English for My Mom,* Muriel Stanek

- *Let's Talk About When Your Parent Doesn't Speak English,* Maureen Wittbold
- *Cooper's Lesson,* Sung Yung Shin
- *I Hate English,* Ellen Levine
- *Scripts of the World,* Suzanne Bukiet
- *The Upside Down Boy/El Niño de Cabeza,* Juan Felipe Herrera
- *Don't Say Ain't,* Irene Smalls
- *Pepita Talks Twice/Pepita Habla Dos Veces,* Ofelia Dumas Lachtman
- *Ashok by Any Other Name,* Sandra Yamate
- *My Name Is Yoon,* Yansook Choi

Write a reaction to the literature you have chosen. Address the following questions:
- What were your thoughts about the language/culture before your reading?
- Did those thoughts change after your reading? If so, how?
- Did you learn anything new about the language/culture? What, if anything, surprised you?

 Internet Connection

The Center for Applied Linguistics

An invaluable resource on topics such as bilingual education, Ebonics and dialects, immigrant education, K–12 ESL, and public policy issues. Contains a searchable database of tests in over 70 languages and an online directory of ESL resources, as well as access to the Education Resources Information Center (ERIC) documents on language learning. Visit the "Ask the Language Experts" page for a list of frequently asked questions and answers.
http://www.cal.org

Activities for ESL Students

A huge database of online or downloadable activities for ESL students. Includes grammar and vocabulary quizzes, crossword puzzles, and more. Also contains bilingual quizzes in 35 languages. (Note: some of the interactive quizzes require JavaScript or Flash player to function correctly.)
http://a4esl.org

Ethnologue—Languages of the World

An excellent searchable database of the world's more than 6,800 known languages. Included is a description of each language population, region, alternate

names, dialects, and a bibliography for further information. Also a Lingua Links library (under "Software" link) with references on topics such as language learning and sociolinguistics.
http://www.ethnologue.com

Indigenous Language Institute

Information about indigenous and endangered languages in the Americas. Browse the collection of personal stories regarding native languages or search the endangered language database.
http://www.indigenous-language.org

References and Recommended Reading

Ada, A. F. (1997, May). Presentation Made to Teachers and Writers, Project Pluma Seminar, New York.

Anzaldua, G. (1999). *Borderlands/La frontera: The new meztiza.* San Francisco: CA: Aunt Lute Books.

Betances, S. (1986). My people made it without bilingual education—What's wrong with your people? *Official Journal of the California School Boards Association, 4*(7), 15.

Castañeda, A. (1996). Language and other lethal weapons: Cultural politics and the rites of children as translators of culture. In A. Gordon & C. Newfield, (Eds.), *Mapping multiculturalism* (pp. 201–213). Minneapolis, MN: University of Minnesota Press.

Collier, V. P., & Thomas, W. P. (1989). How quickly can immigrants become proficient in school English? *Journal of Educational Issues of Language Minority Students, 5,* 26–38.

Corson, D. (2001). *Language diversity and education.* Mahwah, NJ: Lawrence Erlbaum Associates.

Crawford, J. (2000). *At war with diversity: U.S. language policy in an age of anxiety.* Buffalo, NY: Multilingual Matters.

Cummins, J. (1979). Cognitive/academic language proficiency, linguistic interdependence, the optimum age question and some other matters. *Working Papers on Bilingualism, 19,* 121–129.

Cummins, J. (1991). Interdependence of first- and second-language proficiency in bilingual children. In E. Bialystok (Ed.), *Language processes in bilingual children* (pp. 70–89). Cambridge, UK: Cambridge University Press.

Cummins, J. (2001). *Language, power and pedagogy: Bilingual children in the crossfire.* Buffalo, NY: Multilingual Matters.

Delpit, L. (1995). *Other people's children: Cultural conflict in the classroom.* New York: New Press.

Delpit, L. (Ed.). (2003). *The skin that we speak: Thoughts on language and culture in the classroom.* New York: New Press.

Diaz Soto, L. (2002). *Making a difference in the lives of bilingual/bicultural children.* New York: Peter Lang.

Dueñas González, R. (Ed.). (2001). *Language ideologies: Critical perspectives on the official English movement.* Mahwah, NJ: Lawrence Erlbaum Associates.

Freire, P. (2003). *Pedagogy of the oppressed.* New York: Continuum.

Goldstein, T. (2003). *Teaching and learning in a multilingual school: Choices, risks, and dilemmas.* Mahwah, NJ: Lawrence Erlbaum Associates.

Grosjean, F. (1984). *Life with two languages.* Cambridge, MA: Harvard University Press.

Harding, E., & Riley, P. (1999). *The bilingual family: A handbook for parents.* New York: Cambridge University Press.

Igoa, C. (1995). *The inner world of the immigrant child.* Mahwah, NJ: Lawrence Erlbaum Associates.

Jones, G. (1999). *Strange talk: The politics of dialect literature in Gilded Age America.* Berkeley: CA: University of California Press.

Kanno, Y. (2003). *Negotiating bilingual and bicultural identities: Japanese returnees betwixt two worlds.* Mahwah, NJ: Lawrence Erlbaum Associates.

Kim, M. S. (2002). *Non-western perspectives on human communication: Implications for theory and practice.* Thousand Oaks, CA: Sage.

Koda, K. (1994). Second language reading research: Problems and possibilities. *Applied Psycholinguistics, 15,* 1–28.

Mangam, M. (1995). *Building cross-cultural competence: A handbook for teachers.* Chicago: Illinois State Board of Education, Educational Equity Services.

McKay, S. L., & Wong, S. C. (Eds.). (2000). *New immigrants in the United States: Readings for second language educators.* New York: Cambridge University Press.

Nieto, S. (1992). *Affirming diversity: The socio-political context of multicultural education.* White Plains, NY: Longman.

Nieto, S. (2002). *Language, culture, and teaching: Critical perspectives for a new century,* Mahwah, NJ: Lawrence Erlbaum Associates.

Olson, L. (2001). *And still we speak . . . Stories of communities sustaining and reclaiming language and culture.* Oakland, CA: California Tomorrow.

Pérez, B., (Ed.). (2004). *Sociocultural contexts of language and literacy.* Mahwah, NJ: Lawrence Erlbaum Associates.

Phillipson, R. (2000). *Rights to language: Equity, power and education.* Mahwah, NJ: Lawrence Erlbaum Associates.

Pugach, M. (1998). *On the border of opportunity: Education, community, and language at the U.S.–Mexico line.* Mahwah, NJ: Lawrence Erlbaum Associates.

Santa Ana, O. (2004). *Tongue-tied: The lives of multilingual children in public education.* New York: Rowman & Littlefield.

Skutnabb-Kangas, T. (2000). *Linguistic genocide in education or worldwide diversity and human rights?* Mahwah, NJ: Lawrence Erlbaum Associates.

Wong-Fillmore, L. (1991). When learning a second language means losing the first. *Early Childhood Research Quarterly, 6*(3), 323–346.

Gender and
Gender Roles

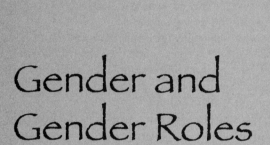

A Place to Begin

What does it mean to be a woman? To be man? Are these identities formed by one's environment or one's biology? Whatever role you feel gender plays in one's position in society, it is important to understand how these identities affect one's experience of school—both as a student and as a teacher.

Just as children enter the classroom with cultural information in their "invisible knapsack," they arrive in school with a gender identity that affects the way they see their peers, their own talents and abilities, and even their role in school. Schools often reinforce these identities with curriculum, school rules, and social activities, and even in teacher–student interactions.

As early as birth, we learn to pay attention to gender. Consider the birth of a child. Assuming that the parents were not told the baby's gender prior to birth, the first question that friends and family ask once the baby is born is undoubtedly, "Is it a boy or a girl?" We want to know this information before all else, as it affects the ways in which we will interact with the child.

Children's literature is also replete with gender-specific messages. Most of the traditional folk and fairytales that form a part of our collective consciousness contain subtle (and not-so-subtle) references to gender-appropriate behavior and roles. For example, in "Little Red Riding Hood," the little girl is frightened by the male wolf, who has eaten her grandmother. The girl is demure and obedient, and serves in a caregiver role by bringing food to her grandmother. The wolf is aggressive, dangerous, and powerful and plays a dominating role in the story. Although we must be mindful of any particular story's historical and cultural background, still we might question the norms we maintain by sharing such a story with young children.

However, before we as educators decide to ban all nursery rhymes and fairytales from the classroom for gender inequity, humorists, such as James Garner in his series *Politically Correct Bedtime Stories,* help us to see the other end of the continuum. Read this excerpt from his version of the Frosty the Snowman story, "Frosty the Persun of Snow" (Garner, 1995, pp. 13–14):

> Bobby said angrily, "When I make a snowman, he always has a corncob pipe!"
>
> "What do you mean?" Betty answered. "This was my idea, and I say it's a snowwommon!"
>
> "But it's shaped like a man!" said Bobby.
>
> "Only to a phallocentric world view like yours!" said Betty.
>
> "How can it be a wommon if we use the old top hat? Womyn don't wear top hats!"
>
> "Oh yeah? What about Marlene Dietrich?" . . .
>
> "It seems like such a silly argument," it continued, "especially since you neglected to give me any private parts."
>
> Betty regained her composure quickly. "I don't care if you were born only an instant ago," she said. "How can you be so naïve as to think a persun's gender is determined by their physical equipment? It's a cultural issue, first and foremost."
>
> "If you want to get huffy," retorted the newcomer, "tell me why you were going to assign me a gender without asking me my preference first."

Betty's face reddened at her insensitivity.

"So what do you prefer?" asked Bobby.

"After watching the way you two communicate, I prefer neither. I think I'd like to be called a 'persun of snow.'"

Think about the spelling changes in this passage (i.e., *wommon, womyn, persun*). Have you seen these words before? How do you feel when you see the changed spellings? What do you think the changes are supposed to represent?

Do you agree with Betty that gender is a cultural issue, or with the persun of snow, that it is based on one's "physical equipment?" What makes you think one way or another?

Another common example of the maintenance of societal gender roles in school involves shop and home economics classes. At one time in American schools, boys took shop where they built things while girls went to their home economics class for sewing and cooking. These curricular choices helped to maintain the hegemony of men in the workplace and women at home with the children. In today's society, boys and girls are more free to learn both carpentry and the gastronomic arts.

But these differences can still be seen in some core subjects, such as math and the sciences. It has long been assumed that boys and girls have different academic strengths, with boys being more adept at science and math and girls having a predilection for humanities-related coursework. While this stereotype may be changing, data from the National Science Foundation show that the change is slow. Consider these two charts:

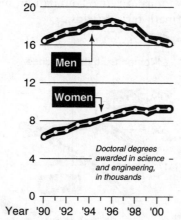

Doctoral Degrees in the Sciences

Source: National Science Foundation *(http://www.nsf.gov).*

Women in the Sciences

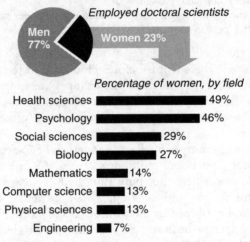

Employed doctoral scientists

Percentage of women, by field

Health sciences	49%
Psychology	46%
Social sciences	29%
Biology	27%
Mathematics	14%
Computer science	13%
Physical sciences	13%
Engineering	7%

Source: National Science Foundation *(http://www.nsf.gov).*

In the first chart, we see that in the last decade of the twentieth century women received between one quarter to one half the number of engineering and science degrees. In the second chart, we learn about the domination of men in these fields in the private sector. Women hold fewer than one quarter of the science and engineering jobs in the workplace, with men occupying 77 percent of these positions.

The good news is that, through school-based initiatives and efforts of organizations such as the National Science Foundation, more and more girls are moving into science- and math-related fields.

Women Studying Science

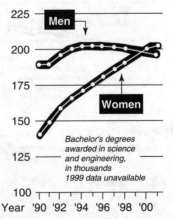

Bachelor's degrees awarded in science and engineering, in thousands
1999 data unavailable

Year '90 '92 '94 '96 '98 '00

Source: National Science Foundation *(http://www.nsf.gov).*

There are more women pursuing bachelor's degrees in a variety of science-related fields in college. The change has been slow, but it seems that the tide is turning in relation to stereotypes about appropriate fields of study for both genders.

Along with messages received in the curriculum, children learn gender roles from interactions with peers and with teachers. For example, every teacher has experienced students in the classroom who are prone to chatting with their neighbors and demonstrating "off-task" behaviors. However, observational studies have shown that teachers tend to tolerate this behavior more from girls than from boys and thus reprimand boys more than girls in this situation. On the other hand, in classroom questioning, boys are often asked more thought-provoking and open-ended questions, while girls are asked more simple yes/no questions (Sadker & Sadker, 1994). What do these habits reveal about stereo typical images of the capabilities of boys versus girls?

Messages about gender roles also frequently become entangled with more overt displays of identity, such as clothing, hairstyles, and the way one moves and speaks. Though we may not state them out loud, we have fairly specific rules in our heads for the ways in which boys and girls should look and behave. For instance, boys should not wear skirts and girls should not have very short hair. Our ideas of what is "masculine" and "feminine" are deeply engrained, though they often reside in our subconscious minds. They are also deeply intertwined with other elements of one's identity such as race, sexual orientation, and even religion. Consider this prose poem about an American Muslim woman who chooses to wear her *hijabi* (traditional Muslim headscarf):

Hijabi

They tell her that she is primitive. They say she should be proud of her femininity, her womanness. They tell her to embrace her sexuality. They tell her a lot of things she does not hear.

"This is who I am."

I think of how easily I abandoned my prayers, my history, the day the planes hit. I remember how I vowed never to fast another day, never to utter another word of prayer, how I told my sister to remove the "Free Palestine" sticker from the bumper of her car.

But here is a woman, an American, a Moslem, who has decided to wear her faith around her face, who has decided that now more than ever, she must not run, but remain steadfast and true.

No, she is not subdued. She is not weakened. She is not compromised.

She is grace. She is mystery. She is humility and strength in the face of so much criticism, of so many unspoken judgments and questions, the stares in the subway, the suffocating heat in the summer afternoons.

I find that my memory of her hair is beginning to fade. Was it brown or black? Falling fast or curling in waves? I think I will never know that part of her again and I am gladdened by this gift of mystery. Now there is only her radiant smile. Her piercing eyes. The defiant affirmation of her truest self.

In the first stanza of the poem, the poet implies that by wearing her *hijabi*, the woman is somehow shunning her femininity, her sexuality. Do you agree with this interpretation? Note the words that the author uses to describe the woman: *grace, mystery, humility,* and *strength*. Are these words that you normally associate with a particular gender? What do you think the author means by the last line, "The defiant affirmation of her truest self?" Take a moment to think about what being male and female means to you at this point in time. Think about these issues as you read the following narrative.

NARRATIVE 16

Before You Read

What role do hair and clothing play in establishing gender identity? How do the boys and girls in your school express their gender identity?

Are there any students in your school who dress in ways not common for their gender, or who have adopted an androgynous look in either dress or hairstyle? How are these students treated in school? How do they interact with their peers? What, if any, assumptions do teachers and other students make about them?

The Most Important Haircut

I remember that day like it was yesterday. It was the longest seven hours and the most terrible day of my life. I had hoped everything would be perfect. It was September and I was going to start a new school. Long Island was new to me and very different from Korea, my home for the first 15 years of my life. The problem started simply because of appearance; I did not look like a girl. My hair was very short like a boy's, and also my clothing was androgynous, jeans and a T-shirt. My intention was not to look like a boy, but rather to make a statement against what I considered unnecessary rules. When I went to high school in Korea, my school was an all-girls' school. It was a very strict school, especially with regard to our appearance. Students had to have long straight hair and we had to wear a uniform skirt. That's why, before I left Korea, I cut my hair very short. I hated silly, rigid rules: why must girls have long hair and wear skirts? I hated stereotyped roles for girls and boys. So I cut my hair.

A few months later, I moved to America with my short hair. I could feel that my American peers had stereotyped me in more categories than being Asian. Based on my appearance, everyone assumed I was a boy. No one took the time to talk to me or know anything about me.

My first period class was photography. The teacher arranged us in groups of two and I was paired with another girl. The girl startled me when she asked, "Why do you look like a girl?"

I was surprised. "I am a girl," I replied without hesitating.

She looked at me curiously and asked, "Then why do you have such short hair?" I could not answer that. Actually, I wanted to say something to explain, but I could not. I lacked the English to express myself and so I had to be mute.

After photo class, I went to the gym for my next period. The physical education teacher introduced himself and gave me a lock. I did not know where the locker rooms were because I was a new student. He told me to go straight through the blue door. I went to the locker room and chose my locker but I felt strange. Maybe it was due to the sweaty smell and pungent odor of deodorant—I had never related that aroma to girls. When I turned back, I saw a scene that shocked me. What was going on? I saw a boy's bathroom. What was I doing here?, I wondered. I ran out of the locker room, but I had no confidence to say, "I am a girl, not a boy!" to my teacher.

Every time I went to period two, the students talked about me. Was I a girl or a boy? I became an attraction in the hallway. Passing students stared and discussed my gender incessantly. I even got a letter in my chemistry class inquiring about my gender preference. I wanted to ignore them but I could not. If I didn't answer their questions, they would label me more and more. I was sad when they continued with remarks about my appearance but I remained silent—partially because I had to; I did not have enough English to tell them all how I was feeling.

After some time, when it was clear that I couldn't answer because of my lack of English, some students began to help me. When we would meet in the hallway, they would call my name and say "hi" to me. I used to hate them. Now, I am thankful to them. I still hated the physical education teacher who gave me the boy's lock and sent me to the wrong locker room, though. I felt so misunderstood by that teacher!

A few months later, when I finally told my PE teacher about that incident, he was so sorry, he hugged me. If I harbored hurt feelings, I would have insisted that I wanted to go back to Korea. But I endured and now am a part of my school community. I have friends and I have confidence about my appearance. I thought I was cutting my hair to defy a rule, but what I was actually doing was building character and strength. It might have been the most important haircut I ever got!

Questions to Consider

1. The author describes her clothing as androgynous. What clothes do we associate with boys only? With girls only? What happens in your school when a student tries to wear clothing that is not traditionally worn by her or his gender?

2. In what way does the narrator's lack of English language proficiency exacerbate the situation? What might she have said to explain her appearance had she been able to articulate her thoughts?

3. The narrator explains that the physical education teacher felt sorry about his mistake and that he ended up hugging the girl. How would you have reacted? Have you ever made a similar mistake in your teaching career?

4. Teachers can be unsure about a student's gender, especially if the student's name is unfamiliar. How would you find out more about a student's gender/identity if you were unsure?

5. Why does the author describe her haircut as "the most important haircut (she) ever got?"

NARRATIVE 17

Before You Read

What does it mean to be a woman? To be a man? What rules are in place for each of these genders with regard to clothing? Physical traits? Professions and jobs? What happens when a person breaks those rules in some way?

Are there any students in your school who behave in ways that are considered "inappropriate" for their gender? In what ways do they "break the rules?" What messages are they being sent by adults and their peers about their "transgression?"

Boys Will Be Boys

I was working with a group of special education children, all of whom had complicated personal and educational needs. One of the children, a little boy named Robert, was living with loving foster parents. At 10 years old, he expressed a wish to bring his mom's purse to school, and also to wear her clothes. He liked to walk on his tiptoes, and had a high, light laugh—more like a giggle.

The parents, concerned for Robert's safety, asked the help of the school psychologist and a private therapist. They did not want the child getting hurt or ridiculed by other students because some of his behavior was deemed effeminate.

One of Robert's teachers would scold him for laughing "like a girl." The school psychologist asked why he liked to walk on his toes. He didn't answer. The private therapist discouraged Robert from bringing his mother's purse to school.

By the time I got involved, Robert—who already had a plateful of other issues—didn't know how to behave, and was shutting down.

My first goal was to reeducate the staff and psychiatrists, and reassure Robert's parents that he could be safe without squelching any of his more effeminate characteristics.

Within Robert's small class of eight students, he was not picked on or ridiculed in any way for his femininity. One of the boys came to school one year for Halloween dressed in drag. He was a popular boy, and everyone told him how pretty he was. We used the opportunity to open up a discussion in the classroom by asking, "Why don't boys dress like girls every day?" and by asking the children to decide which games and toys were for boys, which for girls. They found many exceptions—even dolls didn't count as only for girls, as they had a few action figures in the classroom.

A second opportunity to discuss gender came up when one day one of the boys, who was having a hard time, asked, "Am I ever going to be normal?" And again, I asked the students to talk about what "normal" meant to them. The boy who had originally asked the question said he wanted to know if he would get married and have children and if only "normal" people have children. At the end of the conversation, Robert piped in: "I'm going to open a hair salon with a French name and I don't care about normal." Luckily, Robert's classmates accept him and we have been able to have some important discussions about gender. Unfortunately, there are still those who would like to see Robert act "normal." I am worried for him as he moves on to another class, another school, and out into a world that has very clear rules about what it means to be a "real man" or a "real woman."

Questions to Consider

1. What is gender? Is it "natural?" Would it bother you if a boy wanted to carry a purse or play with dolls? If a girl to wanted to build things and play with guns or cars? Why or why not?

2. How would you help a student like Robert to be safe in the classroom, while expressing himself as he wanted to? What would you do in the classroom to foster acceptance for him?

3. Why was it okay for the popular boy in Robert's class to dress in drag for Halloween, but it wasn't okay for Robert to walk on his tiptoes? How is this message of acceptance conveyed?

4. Make two lists, one of behaviors that are acceptable for men and one for women. Do you or someone you know ever exhibit behaviors or traits that are considered more appropriate for the other gender? If so, what are people's reactions? How do those reactions make you feel?

5. Why do you think the children accepted Robert's behavior in a way the adults in the situation did not?

Project and Extension Activities

1. Look at these cartoons from the comic "Jane's World":

Think about the elements of one's physical appearance that relate to one's gender identity. In the first cartoon, Jane is upset because she is called "sir." In the next frame, she points to her chest in an effort to clarify the situation. How do you think she feels when the clerk does not understand her point?

In the second cartoon, two men discuss another woman's choice of hairstyle. After having read "The Most Important Haircut," do you agree with the statement "Women take their hair *soooo* seriously?" Why or why not? How do you feel about women who choose to wear their hair very short?

Write a list of the physical characteristics that you feel "make" one a man or a woman. Ask a member of the opposite gender to share their own list with you. Compare your answers. Do any of the items on the other person's list surprise you? Order your list by putting the characteristic most important to you at the top, with the least important on the bottom. Compare your lists again.

2. Do the following action research in your classroom:
   Quantitative research:
   a. Keep track of the number of times you call on girls and boys during the course of one class period or one lesson.
   b. How often do you respond to off-task behavior for boys? For girls?
   Graph the results using a bar chart or other graphic organizer. Do the results surprise you at all?
   Qualitative research:
   a. Identify the types of questions (open-ended, yes/no questions, opinion questions, etc.) you ask boys and girls.
   b. How do you respond to girls and boys in class? For example: with a nod, with praise, with elaboration and extension questions, etc. Are your responses generally different for each gender?
   Write a description of one particular incident that is typical of your interactions with boys and one for girls.

3. What gender-specific terms do we use in everyday speech? Write a list of as many terms as come to mind. Here are a few to start you off:
   • Actor/actress
   • Wife/husband
   • Waiter/waitress

- Nurse/male nurse
- Congressman/congressperson

Which of these terms are considered unacceptable in today's society? Why do you think they are now inappropriate? Which ones do you find particularly offensive? Which ones do not bother you? Why?

4. At the beginning of this chapter, we looked at several charts with data regarding the number of women involved in the fields of science and engineering. How do you feel about the role of women in these fields? Write a brief statement about your opinion.

    Now visit the Project Implicit website (*https://implicit.harvard.edu/implicit/*). Once there, click on the "Demonstration" link. Once you agree to enter the site, you will be directed to a page with a choice for a variety of tests. Click on the link, "Go to the Demonstration Tests," then on "Gender-Science IAT." This test is meant to measure if you have any implicit preference for linking males with science and females with liberal arts. Take the test and view how your answers are interpreted by the program. Are you surprised by the results? Write a brief reaction to the test and about your results.

5. Who are today's male role models? Female role models? Survey your students to find out. What do the top role models for each gender say about what it means to be a man? To be a woman? Compare the role models you had as a child to those of your students. What differences do you see?

6. According to the Human Rights Campaign Foundation (2005), the following states have laws, judicial rulings, statutes, or administrative orders prohibiting discrimination in employment based on gender identity:

    California
    Connecticut
    Florida
    Hawaii
    Illinois
    Kentucky
    Massachusetts
    Minnesota
    New Jersey
    New Mexico
    New York
    Pennsylvania
    Rhode Island

Is your state on the list? What might such a ruling look like for your school? With your students' help, write a proclamation banning gender identity discrimination for your classroom. As an exercise, extend the range of your classroom proclamation to cover your entire school. Identify current practices that both support and violate your new proclamation.

7. Look at the cartoon at the start of this chapter. What traits or talents do you associate with being "feminine" or female? Which ones do you associate with

being "masculine" or male? Think about someone you know, either personally or in the public eye, who does not fit these gender stereotypes. If someone you know, interview them about their life in relation to these gender
roles. If someone famous or unapproachable, write a list of possible interview
questions and then brainstorm what their answers might be.

Cultural Exploration

1. *Explore video:* Watch the film, *Gender Equity in the Classroom,* WGBY-TV,
   Springfield, MA (*http://wgby.org/edu/gender/guide.html*). Choose an issue in
   the film that is important for your school context. Would the suggestions
   made in the film work in your school? Why or why not?
      Design a lesson for your students about a gender issue. Write a brief
   lesson plan including handouts, references, and teaching suggestions. If
   possible, share your lesson plan with your students, colleagues, and school
   leadership.
2. *Explore people:* Interview a male student who in your opinion represents the
   stereotype of masculinity and a female student who represents the stereotype of femininity. Address the following questions in your interview:
   • What does it mean to be a male/female student in this school?
   • What elements of your identity as a male/female student are most impor-
     tant to you? How do you show your maleness/femaleness in school?
   • Does being a male/female affect your academic performance? Your social
     interactions? Your relationship with your teachers? If so, in what ways?
   • Was there ever a time when you were keenly aware of your gender in a
     school situation? What happened? How did you feel?
   • Did you ever experience prejudice or discrimination due to your gender
     in school? Please describe the incident.
   Using the answers to these and other questions from your interview, write a
   brief biography of each person. Share them with your interviewees and ask
   for feedback as to their accuracy.
3. *Explore literature:* Choose to read about a gender issue that interests you, or
   one that you know little about.

Novels, Short Stories, Memoirs: choose one

   • *Ain't I a Woman,* bell hooks
   • *Larque on the Wing,* Nancy Springer
   • *The Last Time I Wore a Dress,* Daphne Scholinski

- *Female Masculinity,* Judith Halberstam
- *Gender Shock: Exploding the Myths of Male and Female,* Phyllis Burke

Young Adult Literature: choose two

- *Every Girl Tells a Story: A Celebration of Girls Speaking Their Minds,* Carolyn Jones
- *Gutsy Girls: Young Women Who Dare,* Tina Schwager & Michele Schuerger
- *Sugar in the Raw: Voices of Young Black Girls in America,* Rebecca Carroll
- *Shabanu: Daughter of the Wind,* Suzanne Fisher Staples
- *History of Women in Science for Young People,* Vivian Sheldon Epstein
- *Athletic Shorts,* Chris Crutcher
- *The Teenage Guy's Survival Guide,* Jeremy Daldry

Picturebooks: Choose three

- *Drum, Chavi, Drum!/;Toca, Chavi, Toca!,* Mayra Dole
- *Sarah, Plain and Tall,* Patricia MacLachlan
- *Ramona the Brave,* Beverly Cleary
- *Millicent Kwan: Girl Genius,* Lisa Yee
- *The Adventures of Sparrowboy,* Brian Pinkney
- *Henry's Baby,* Mary Hoffman
- *Like Jake and Me,* Mavis Jukes
- *Boys at Work,* Gary Soto

Write a reaction to the literature you have chosen. Address the following questions:
- What were your thoughts about the issue before your reading?
- Did those thoughts change after your reading? If so, how?
- Did you learn anything new about the issue? What, if anything, surprised you?

Internet Connection

The Mid-Atlantic Equity Consortium

Click on the "Gender Equity Programs and Services" link in the center of the homepage for a list of resources, including articles such as, "Beyond Title IX: Gender Equity Issues in Schools," fact sheets such as, "Adolecent Boys: Statistics and Trends," and an excellent gender equity handbook entitled, "It's Your Right!" *http://www.maec.org*

National Transgender Advocacy Coalition

Read about current research initiatives, success stories, statistics, legal issues, gender studies, and lobby efforts. Of particular interest is the Bill of Gender Rights and printable media information kits and fact sheets.
http://www.ntac.org/

American Association of University Women

Of particular interest are the research studies on girls and education (click on the "Research" tab at the top of the page). Titles include "Beyond the Gender Wars," "Girls in the Middle," "How Schools Shortchange Girls," "Hostile Hallways," and a sexual harassment guide. On the site you can find information about advocacy and sign up for a "get the facts" email alert.
http://www.aauw.org

Girls Inc.

Under the "Find Resources" tab on the "About Girls Inc." page, you will find a list of fact and resource sheets such as, "Tips for Adults to Help Girls Achieve Rights" and "The Girls' Bill of Rights." There is also an interactive quiz regarding facts about the status of women and girls in today's society.
http://www.girlsinc.org

The National Organization for Men Against Sexism

This organization describes itself as "pro-feminist," "gay-affirmative," and "anti-racist." Under the "Resources" link is an excellent downloadable "citebase"—a database of citations and statistics with references on issues of sexism and bias-based violence.
http://www.nomas.org

References and Recommended Reading

Belenky, M. F., Clinchy, B. M., Goldberger, N. R., & Tarule, J. M. (1986). *Women's ways of knowing: The development of self, voice and mind.* New York: Basic Books.

Bettis, P., & Adams, N. (Eds.). (2005). *Geographies of girlhood: Identities in-between.* Mahwah, NJ: Lawrence Erlbaum Associates.

Fausto-Sterling, A. (2000). *Sexing the body: Gender politics and the construction of sexuality.* New York: Basic Books.

Freire, P. (2003). *Pedagogy of the oppressed.* New York: Continuum.

Frye, M. (1992). *Race, class and gender in the United States.* New York: St. Martin's.

Garner, J. F. (1995). *Politically correct holiday stories.* New York: Macmillan.

Glennon, W. (1999). *200 ways to raise a girl's self esteem.* Boston: Conari.

Glennon, W. (2000). *200 ways to raise a boy's emotional intelligence.* Boston: Conari.

Gore, J. M., (1993). *The struggle for pedagogies: Critical and feminist discourses as regimes of truth.* New York: Routledge.

Harris Scholastic Research. (1993). *Hostile hallways: The AAUW survey on sexual harassment in America's schools.* Washington, DC: American Association of University Women Foundation.

Human Rights Campaign Foundation. (2005). *The state of the workplace for lesbian, gay, bisexual and transgender people.* Washington, DC: Author.

Kindlon, D., & Thompson, M. (2000). *Raising Cain: Protecting the emotional life of boys.* New York: Ballantine.

Kleinfeld, J., & Yerian, S. (1995). *Gender tales: Tensions in the schools.* Mahwah, NJ: Lawrence Erlbaum Associates.

Lorber, J. (1994). *Paradoxes of gender.* New Haven: Yale University Press.

Maher, F., & Ward, J. (2002). *Gender and teaching.* Mahwah, NJ: Lawrence Erlbaum Associates.

Morris Schaffer, S., & Perlman Gordon, L. (2000). *Why boys don't talk and why we care: A mother's guide to connection.* Chevy Chase, MD: Mid-Atlantic Equity Consortium.

Okin, S. M., Cohen, J., Howard, M., & Nussbaum, M. C. (1999). *Is multiculturalism bad for women?* Princeton, NJ: Princeton University Press.

O'Reilly, P., Penn, E., & deMarrais, K. (2001). *Educating young adolescent girls.* Mahwah, NJ: Lawrence Erlbaum Associates.

Pipher, M. (1994). *Reviving Ophelia: Saving the selves of adolescent girls.* New York: Ballantine.

Romaine, S. (1999). *Communicating gender.* Mahwah, NJ: Lawrence Erlbaum Associates.

Sadker, M., & Sadker, D. (1994). *Failing at fairness: How our schools cheat girls.* New York: Touchstone.

Sanders, J., Koch, J., & Urso, J. (1997). *Gender equity right from the start.* Mahwah, NJ: Lawrence Erlbaum Associates.

Tannen, D. (1990). *You just don't understand: Women and men in conversation.* New York: Ballantine.

Tannen, D. (1994). *Talking from 9 to 5: Women and men in the workplace: Language, sex and power.* New York: Avon.

Taylor, D., & Lorimer, M. (2002). Helping boys succeed. *Educational Leadership, 60*(4), 68–70.

Thorne, B. (1993). *Gender play: Girls and boys in school.* Piscataway, NJ: Rutgers University Press.

Learning (Dis)Abilities and Special Needs

A Place to Begin

We have all heard the term *special education,* and most likely have worked with students with special needs. Public Law 94–142, the Individuals with Disabilities Act (IDEA) defines a *learning disability* in the following way:

> . . . a disorder in one or more of the basic psychological processes involved in understanding or in using language, spoken or written, that may manifest itself in an imperfect ability to listen, think, speak, read, write, spell, or do mathematical calculations, including conditions such as perceptual disabilities, brain injury, minimal brain dysfunction, dyslexia, and developmental aphasia.

To meet the diverse needs of students with learning disabilities, an Individualized Education Plan (IEP) for each eligible student is frequently created by school leadership in what is known as a Committee on Special Education (CSE). These committees commonly include the student's teachers, special education professionals, parents and/or caregivers, and sometimes even the student. An IEP sets short- and long-term goals for the student, and establishes a series of appropriate accommodations and modifications based on the student's disability. The IEP is an important document for teachers as it helps them to work more effectively with the child.

Many different types of learning disabilities fall under the heading of special education. The two main categories are as follows (Idonline.org, 2005):

- *Developmental speech and language disorders:* People with these types of disorders have trouble producing speech sounds, understanding what others are saying, or communicating meaning in spoken language (developmental articulation disorder is one example).
- *Academic skills disorders:* Those who display these skills disorders demonstrate significant delays in reading, writing, or mathematical skills (dyslexia is an example of an academic reading disorder).

Two other important disabilities that affect many schoolage children, as well as adults, are Attention Deficit Disorder (ADD) and Attention-Deficit/Hyperactivity Disorder (ADHD). Individuals with ADD demonstrate an inability to concentrate and/or to remain still for long periods of time. They may be easily distracted from a task, inattentive in class, and overly spontaneous. When these symptoms are accompanied by hyperactivity, the disorder is called ADHD.

The cartoon at the start of this chapter depicts a child who is being treated for ADHD (as evidenced by his mother's statement regarding the drug Ritalin—a common medication for ADHD). The mother is concerned that her son can't seem to focus on anything, yet the boy's daily schedule posted on the refrigerator provides a clue as to at least part of the problem. Do you have any students who have been diagnosed with ADD or ADHD? How do they behave in the classroom? What is done in your community to help these students succeed in school?

NARRATIVE 18

Before You Read

Think about what it is like to work with students who have a learning disability. Are these students mainstreamed in your school, or are they separated? How might a school for students with learning disabilities differ from a school with a mix of learning disabled and non-learning disabled students? What might a classroom in each school look like?

Do you or someone you know have a learning disability? How does this challenge shape you or that person? Do you think that a teacher with a learning disability is better able to work with students with learning disabilities? Why or why not?

The Kilmurray School

The Kilmurray School is a boarding school for dyslexic students. It was also my first teaching position, my first job after college, and it changed me.

When I arrived at Kilmurray, I was 22 years old, drowning in debt, and uncertain about my future. I had no previous teaching experience. I did not even have an education degree to my name. I felt lost. I felt as if I had shed a great deal of my identity leaving college. If I was no longer a college student, no longer a literature major, no longer a member of student government—what was I?

I expected that I would begin to define myself again once I started working. I thought this was the next step to becoming an adult. Instead, Kilmurray showed me two aspects of myself, of my identity, that had always been within me but that I had never confronted. The first aspect I realized was my own learning disability—dyslexia. It had always been a part of me that I fiercely denied and repressed. The second aspect involved my memories of struggling as a student. Through this new teaching job I was to reconcile myself with those nightmares and remember and relearn what it meant to be a struggling student, troubled with self-doubt and confusion.

I have a learning disability. I've said those words all through my years of schooling, but I have never said them as knowingly or with as much understanding as I say them now after teaching at Kilmurray. I had grown up with the knowledge, but until this point I had spent much of my academic career denying that I had needs or difficulties that were different from anyone else's in my class. I only confessed in extreme circumstances, like when I had to explain my poor spelling to a teacher or during an embarrassing classroom situation. Even though it was painfully clear that I could not spell even some of the simplest words, I often refused help or accommodations. Every time I explained my disability, I felt as if I was taking the "easy way out" of work. I dreaded telling people, and often felt guilty for it. The explanation I had for my learning disability was often short and uninformed since I knew little about it myself. I had no idea that I was about to learn so much about myself working at Kilmurray.

My first three weeks there consisted of training in the Orton-Gillingham method of phonics instruction. I am not sure how to explain what learning phonics was like for me, but I can say that it completely changed how I read. I never knew how poor my reading was until I relearned the sounds of letters. Every lesson about symbols and their relationships to sound was new to me. I did not know that "ea" had three different sounds, as in "eat," "bread," and "steak." I had always gotten by on guesswork. I couldn't even pronounce my short vowels correctly, much less determine which ones happened in certain combinations of letters. For the first time in my life I learned to properly "sound it out."

I was reading words that I had only guessed at or skimmed. I had no idea what I had been missing. Did everyone read like this? Did everyone spell like this? My new abilities were worlds away from where I had started. My father was a teacher and the house was always full of books. How could I have lived so long and known so little about reading?

Everyone in my family was an avid reader. I read all the time for pleasure. I spent four years of college doing almost nothing but reading, yet I never knew that I was missing so much of it. I wondered why I struggled in some courses where the lectures didn't correspond directly to the reading.

During my training I discovered just how badly I had been struggling, and then I wanted nothing more than to read everything. I devoured books with new relish. Sometimes I read just to marvel at my new skill. The newness of reading was highlighted when I went back to Maine to visit my parents. I had heard of Sunoco gas stations before, but I had never recalled seeing any. Driving home after my training I discovered that there were two in my hometown. Until then I had never read those signs.

That was only my first lesson, about the joy of being able to read. The second, a more painful one, was to happen when I began to work with students and relived how awful not knowing how to read can be. I spent a year living with 23 freshman boys. Nearly all had several qualities in common: they were very bright, they were dyslexic, and the combination of the two led them to think very poorly of themselves. They were often terribly awkward and hard on themselves. They were just like me when I went through school.

While at my parents' house, I looked through some of my old paperwork. I found an article one of my teachers had given my parents about children with learning disabilities. I had seen it before but had never studied it. It contained a list of emotional difficulties that often accompanied learning disabilities. For the benefit of my parents, the teacher had underlined several that pertained to me. One was depression, another was perfectionism, and a third was frustration. Somehow I had chosen to forget or at least never think about how rough school was. Now I had to remember because I saw it in my students every day.

Like me, my students suffered from seeing themselves as faulty. They wanted nothing more than to be normal, to read as easily as everyone else, to have nothing wrong with them. I was among boys who were on the road to manhood and hating themselves because, although they knew that they were bright, they were failures in school. Even at a school that was supposed to accommodate for their needs, failure was an ever-present danger in their minds.

I watched while one student kicked in his own stereo system, reducing it splinters and scrap. He said he did it because he was tired of feeling stupid. He was *not* stupid. He was smart and perceptive—so much so that he saw the ease with which others succeeded in school and when he compared his performance to theirs, he found his own faults. To explain the discrepancy, he believed that he must be stupid. This student was really one of the nicest kids I could ever hope to meet, but there is no suffering worse than self-loathing.

Living in that dorm, hearing those woes, I began to recall the times in elementary and middle school I cried over being stupid. I began to recall the outrageous antics I pulled to get attention when I failed.

The student who kicked in his stereo was lashing out in the same way I did when I was his age. Once in grade school I cursed at some kids who were teasing me in gym class and was told to sit by myself in the corner. The students continued to make gestures from across the basketball court, so I stood up and swore at them at the top of my lungs. This exiled me further from my peers, and marked me as a failure in my own eyes, much like my student's experience.

I still wrestle with seeing myself as faulty. It hurts to think that way, especially since I put such a high price on literacy. It has gotten a little easier now that I have studied what learning disabilities are, but it still haunts me when my students correct my spelling or the principal can't bring parents into my classroom because I might have something misspelled on the board from the day's lesson. Until I worked at Kilmurray, I had never accepted parts of me that needed to be addressed, confronted, acknowledged, and healed. I never truly accepted that I have a learning disability. It is a shame that it is a negative label and is looked upon as failure by many people. It is especially painful since my family, my peers, and the culture with which I identify place such a high value on literacy. But I want to "claim ownership" of my disability. It is a part of me, not something wrong with me. And I want my students to know that as well.

Questions to Consider

1. Why do think it took the author so long to "take ownership" of his disability? What might have helped him to acknowledge this part of himself sooner than he did?
2. What are some of the most prominent characteristics of a person with dyslexia, as described in the narrative? Do you know of any others? Have you seen any of these behaviors in students in your classes?
3. Have you ever sent home literature about a student's disability, as the narrator's teacher did? If so, what were your goals in doing so? What kind of feedback (if any) did you receive from the student's home?
4. The narrator mentions that he pulled "outrageous antics" to get attention when he failed. What behavior have you seen in your own students with learning disabilities?
5. The principal in the narrator's school did not like to bring visitors to his classroom because he often had misspellings on the board. In what ways is this policy contradictory to the mission of a school for learning disabled students?

NARRATIVE 19

Before You Read

Think about your school's special education program. Does your school subscribe to the inclusion model? Do you have a co-teaching model, or are students with special needs pulled out of classes for services? How do you feel about the model in place in your school? How do you feel about having special education students in your class? How do your colleagues feel? In what ways, if any, are these feelings manifested in the classroom? The hallways? The teacher's lounge?

"It's Not Fair"

The summer after my junior year in college, I was an intern at a public high school's summer program. My official title was student teacher, but for the first two weeks of my nine-week term I was little more than a glorified paper runner who taught the occasional vocabulary lesson. When my co-teacher asked me if I would be interested in working with students with special needs, I jumped at the chance to do something more meaningful than taking attendance.

He explained that it would be my responsibility to make sure that the accommodations specified on the students' respective IEPs were being met. The summer school had a morning session for freshman students and an afternoon session for upperclassmen. Between the two English classes that we taught, I would be in charge of seven students who had IEPs.

After agreeing to help, I was directed to the special education teacher for more instructions. She was the only such teacher on staff at the summer school and was relieved to hear that I had been sent to help. She elaborated on the kinds of things that I needed to look out for with the students and gave me copies of their IEPs. Some of the students' plans allowed for more time during tests or the use of dictionaries or word processors. I was also responsible for grading their papers and tests, because certain students were not to be penalized for spelling errors. The specialist would be doing my job on a larger scale, checking on students in five classes as compared to my two. She assured me that I could come to her with any questions that I might have and that as long as the students followed their IEPs, things would be fine. I left her room feeling confident. Though I had no experience with special education, I was convinced that I could handle the task of making sure that the students received their individual accommodations. How hard could it be to keep tabs on seven kids?

Around the fourth week of my internship, I began to suspect that my co-teacher had given me the job of overseeing the special education students because he didn't want to be bothered to do it himself. He would say things about the special education teacher coming into our classroom and worrying about the kids too much. He talked about how the students with IEPs were doing compared to their classmates, and once referred to a boy as "hopeless no matter how many answers you give him." I was unsure how to respond. I didn't agree with him, but I also didn't want to tell him how to run his class or what he should think about his students. I kept quiet and decided that his attitude was due to his own personal inexperience with special education. Although he was the supervisor of and teacher at the summer school, his year-long job was as a career counselor. He had not been a classroom teacher in more than 10 years, save summer school sessions. He admitted that he wasn't used to IEPs because in the past when he taught, the special education students were not members of the everyday classroom. The high school's inclusive policy was foreign to him, and in previous summers he let the special education teacher take care of anything extra that the students needed.

As a result of his indifference, things went rather smoothly. I became used to checking with "my" students to make sure that they understood the directions or to see if they needed more time, and he taught the lessons to the entire class. We developed a rhythm and the days started to fly by. In the middle of our fifth week, something happened to make me revisit my uneasiness with my co-teacher's philosophies on special education.

The class was taking a unit test on the book that they'd just finished reading. I was leaving to go to another classroom with three boys who were allotted more time to work. As we were leaving, a female student who'd already been handed her test said, "It's not fair that the stupid kids get to leave and have help on their tests." Though her complaint was directed at me, she intentionally said it loud enough for the whole class to hear. From the looks on the kids' faces, not one person in the room missed her comment except my co-teacher, who was in the back of the room printing out additional copies of the test. Looking around the room, I saw that students' reactions were mixed. Some seemed shocked and confused; others laughed or whispered. The three students with me stopped and stared at her. They looked hurt and embarrassed, uncertain how to react in front of everyone.

They weren't the only ones who were uncertain. I had no idea how to handle it. My first impulse was to shake her for hurting her classmates' feelings. But I could also see that she was frustrated. All of the students in the class were in summer school because they had failed ninth-grade English the first time around. Now the students with IEPs were getting special help and doing much better. For lack of something better to say, I turned to the girl and said, "If you would like to talk to me about getting some special help of your own that's fine, but don't ever call anyone from this class stupid again." With that, I herded the three boys out of the room. I apologized to them for what she said and told them that I was sure that she didn't mean it. The boys didn't look convinced, and stayed pretty quiet the rest of the period. When I got back to the classroom after the test, I approached the girl and asked her if she really did want some help. She replied angrily that she didn't need any.

After classes that afternoon, I brought up the subject with my co-teacher, asking him if he'd heard what went on and what he wanted to do about it. He hadn't heard but said that he was sure that it would blow over. He said that we didn't have enough time to talk about it with the whole class with all of the other things that we had to cover in order to get the students up to speed for next year. Again, though it might not have been the best decision, I backed down and agreed with him to let it go.

Nothing happened the next day as a result of the girl's outburst. The three students whom she'd embarrassed acted as though it hadn't happened and I heard no conversation about it from anyone else in class. The girl didn't mention it either—not that I'd expected her to. She was unusually quiet for a couple days after, and I got the feeling that she felt guilty for hurting her classmates. It seemed that my co-teacher was right, that things did just blow over. But I couldn't forget what had happened and I couldn't help thinking that it was important. Although I was somewhat relieved that no one brought it up, I was also mad that everyone was just taking it for granted as something that just happened and couldn't be helped. It seemed like our collective inaction spoke volumes about the way society ignores and condescends to the special needs of individuals.

Looking back on it, I really wish that my co-teacher and I had had some kind of talk with the class to explain why certain students get extra help with things. I'm afraid that the kids with IEPs internalized their classmate's feelings that they were stupid and being given unfair advantages. And I'm sure that there were some students who, like the girl who spoke out, were confused and angry about the extra attention I was giving their classmates. Even beyond addressing this issue directly with the class, my co-teacher's and my own attitudes toward special education greatly affected the students. By ignoring those students on IEPs and downplaying their disabilities or struggles, he unconsciously encouraged students to resent and misunderstand their classmates. And even though I tried so hard to help the special education students, I unknowingly contributed to their feelings of alienation from the rest of the class.

I treated "my" students as if they were my only students and we were a class unto ourselves. I was unconsciously helping to keep them from feeling a part of the class. The goal of inclusion is to create a community of learners of all abilities, interests, and backgrounds, and the first step to achieving that goal is the teacher's own belief in and understanding of inclusion. I was working against the goal by not seeing the special needs students in the context of the whole class. When I was given the opportunity to work with these students, I stopped thinking about the rest of the members of the class. I was just as guilty as my co-teacher because I was not working to foster the larger community.

Questions to Consider

1. What do you think the narrator's co-teacher meant when he said that the special education teacher "worries about the kids too much?" Do you agree?

2. A lot is revealed about the co-teacher's stance on special needs students' abilities when he says that one boy is "hopeless no matter how many answers you give him." What do you think he means by "hopeless?" How does this statement reflect his misunderstanding about how special education supports work?

3. The narrator remains quiet in two instances in the story. Why do you think she decided not to confront her co-teacher in each instance? Would you have confronted the co-teacher? Why or why not? If so, what would you have said?

4. How did both teachers unconsciously create an environment where a student could say, "It's not fair that the stupid kids get to leave and have help on their tests?" In what ways do you think this students' feelings may be similar to those of both teachers?

5. The narrator wishes that she and her co-teacher would have addressed the girl's comment with the class the following day. What would you have said to the class? To the girl who made the comment?

6. The narrator regrets having unintentionally contributed to the isolation of her special education students. In what ways might she have helped make them more a part of the class?

Project and Extension Activities

1. Look at this cartoon:

INSPIRED BY BEVERLY RAINFORTH

© 1999 MICHAEL F. GIANGRECO. ILLUSTRATION BY KEVIN RUELLE. PEYTRAL PUBLICATIONS, INC. 952-949-8707

THE EVOLUTION OF SWIMMING LESSONS:
SURPRISINGLY SIMILAR TO THE EVOLUTION
OF INCLUDING STUDENTS WITH
DISABILITIES IN GENERAL EDUCATION.

Source: Reprinted from *Flying by the Seat of Your Pants: More Absurdities and Realities of Special Education* (p. 20), by M. F. Giangreco, 1999. Minnetonka, MN: Peytral Publications. Reprinted by permission.

Think about your own school setting. Which of the three illustrations best corresponds to your school program for students with special needs? Create a cartoon that best illustrates your school's special education philosophy.

2. Stereotypical portrayals on television of students with different disabilities are numerous and often offensive. Choose one "offending" TV show and analyze the portrayal of a specific character that you feel is stereotypically represented. Answer the following questions:

- What disability is this character intended to represent?
- What does the character *do* that makes her or him representative of the group?
- How does the character *look* that makes him or her representative of the group?
- In what ways is the character funny? Successful? Intelligent? What are her or his dominant characteristics?
- Do you like this character? Why or why not?

Now interview a person with that disability (Note: your interviewee should have seen the same TV show and be somewhat familiar with the character). Ask the following questions:

- Is this character a valid representation of your disability? If yes, in what ways? If no, why not?
- Do you feel that this character has brought positive or negative attention to your disability? Why?
- If you were given the keys to the TV studio for a day, and were able to create a TV show about your disability, what would your main character be like?

3. Conduct action research in your school, or by visiting a different school. Be a "fly on the wall" by observing an inclusion class or a pull-out special education class for one school day. What accommodations are made for the special education students in the class? Complete the following chart of common accommodations. Describe the instances in which each accommodation is used in the classroom (the first one is done for you as an example):

Accommodation	Activity	Student Information
Preferential seating	Teacher writing notes on the board	Student is seated at the front of the room and taking notes
Extended time for tests		
Notes provided for student		
Spelling is not counted		
Curriculum is modified		
Co-teacher keeps student on task		
Student can use a calculator		
Students can use a scribe		

What do you notice about the activities or lessons? When are accommodations most used? How are they used? How do they seem to help or hinder students?

4. Look at this cartoon:

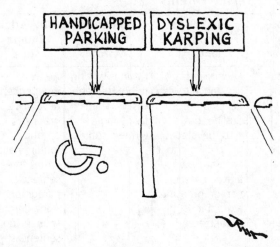

You may know that people with dyslexia tend to reverse letters in their writing. What are some other symptoms of dyslexia? How does it affect one's ability to read? Visit the website for the International Dyslexia Association (*http://www.interdys.org*). Click on the "Educators" link and visit the Frequently Asked Questions (FAQ) page to learn more. Prepare a brief report for your colleagues.

5. Talk to a special education teacher in your school. Ask for a list of recommendations, strategies, and suggestions for working with students with learning disabilities. Check off the strategies that are already a part of your own classroom routine. Develop a plan for incorporating more of the strategies into your teaching.

6. Reporting progress to parents is important for all students, but especially imperative for a student with a learning disability. Look at the sample report on page 168.

   Think about a student in your class with a learning disability. Create a template for reporting home about that student's progress in class. How would you adapt this form to use with all students?

7. Look at the cartoon at the beginning of this chapter. What message is the artist trying to convey? Interview a student with a learning disability about his or her daily activities. Create a list for your student like the one in the cartoon. Are you surprised by the number of tasks in which the student is involved? Follow up your interview by asking the student how she or he feels about having this daily routine.

Annual Goal: Kevin *will* use graphic organizers to write a three-paragraph essay using correct sequencing of sentences including topic sentence, supporting sentences and conclusion.

Reporting Progress to Parents

1st Period Ending November	2nd Period Ending January	3rd Period Ending March	4th Period Ending June	July-August
Kevin is writing three-sentence paragraphs with correct sequencing, including a topic sentence, supporting sentence and conclusion. Objective met.	Kevin needs assistance to develop the outline, but once developed, he follows it to accurately write a five-sentence paragraph using a graphic organizer.	Kevin is writing two-paragraph essays when following a written outline.	Kevin independently develops a graphic organizer (outline) and writes three-sentence paragraphs using correct sequencing of sentences.	

Source: Excerpt from *Sample Individualized Education Program (IEP) and Guidance Document,* New York State Education Department, Office of Vocational and Educational Services for Individuals with Disabilities, December 2002; *http://vesid33.nysed.gov/specialed/publications/policy/iep.* Reprinted by permission.

Cultural Exploration

1. *Explore video:* Watch the film, *How Difficult Can This Be? The F.A.T. City Workshop,* WETA (*http://www.ricklavoie.com/videos.html*). Choose two activities in the film that most remind you of your own students. Describe each activity and its relation to your students.

   Design a simulation for your students that allows them to understand a particular learning disability. Write a brief lesson plan including handouts, references, and teaching suggestions. If possible, share your lesson plan with your students, colleagues, and school leadership.

2. *Explore people:* Interview a student with a learning disability. Address the following questions:
   - What is it like to be a special education student in this school? Do you feel comfortable in all of your classes? Why or why not?
   - What elements of your identity (if any) do you feel you want to hide in school? How does this make you feel?

- How does your learning disability affect your academic performance? Your social interactions? Your relationship with your teachers? In what ways?
- Was there ever an occasion when you completely forgot your learning disability in a school situation? What happened? How did you feel?
- Did you ever experience prejudice or discrimination due to your learning disability in school? Please describe the incident.

Using the answers to these and other questions from your interview, write a brief biography of the person. Share it with your interviewee and ask for feedback as to its accuracy.

3. *Explore literature:* Choose to read about a learning (dis)ability.

Novels, Short Stories, Memoirs: choose one

- *Mothers Talk about Learning Disabilities: Personal Feelings,* Elizabeth Weiss
- *Laughing Allegra: The Inspiring Story of a Mother's Struggle and Triumph Raising a Daughter with Learning Disabilities,* Anne Ford & John-Richard Thompson, Eds.
- *Learning Outside the Lines,* Jonathan Mooney & David Cole
- *Thinking in Pictures: And Other Reports from My Life with Autism,* Temple Grandin
- *Learning Disabilities and Life Stories,* A. Garrod, Pano Rodis, & M. L. Boscardin, Eds.
- *Educating Tigers,* Wendy Sand Eckel

Young Adult Literature: choose two

- *Views from Our Shoes: Growing Up with a Brother or Sister with Special Needs,* Donald J. Meyer, Ed.
- *Adam Zigzag,* Barbara Barrie
- *Egg Drop Blues,* Jacqueline Turner Banks
- *Joey Pigza Swallowed the Key; Joey Pigza Loses Control; What Would Joey Do?,* Jack Gantos
- *Angie,* Pat Bezzant
- *Axe-Time, Sword-Time,* Barbara Corcoran
- *Spaceman,* Jane Cutler
- *Many Ways to Learn: Young People's Guide to Learning Disablities,* Judith M. Stern & U. Ben-Ami
- *Will the Real Gertrude Hollings Please Stand Up?,* Sheila Greenwald
- *The Safe Place,* Tehila Peterseil

Picturebooks: Choose two

- *Adam and the Magic Marble,* Adam Buehrens
- *Ian's Walk,* Laurie Lears

- *Secrets Aren't (Always) for Keeps,* Barbara Aiello
- *The Don't Give Up Kid,* Jeanne Gehret

Write a reaction to the literature you have chosen. Address the following questions:

- What were your thoughts about the learning (dis)ability before your reading?
- Did those thoughts change after your reading? If so, how?
- Did you learn anything new about the learning (dis)ability? What, if anything, surprised you?

 Internet Connection

LD Online—The Interactive Guide to Learning Disabilities

An extensive website about learning disabilities for parents and teachers. Follow the link to the "ABCs of LD" for articles on special education issues for teachers. There is also a section on teaching strategies and a collection of personal narratives by teachers, parents, and students about the challenges of learning disabilities. *http://www.ldonline.org*

Children and Adults with Attention-Deficit/Hyperactivity Disorder

This site provides the visitor with information about advocacy, research, education, and support. Of particular interest is the description of public policy regarding students with ADHD and overview of the possible accommodations for students outlined in American with Disabilities Act (ADA), Individuals with Disabilities Education Act (IDEA), and Section 504. *www.chadd.org*

Learning Disabilities Association of America

Click on the "For Teachers" tab to find information about the different types of learning disabilities, possible symptoms, and strategies for working with students with a learning disability. There are also links to discussions of the social and emotional aspects of learning disabilities. *www.ldanatl.org*

Council for Exceptional Children

View the law regarding the Individuals with Disabilities Education Act and final regulations in its original language. There is a list of topic briefs on the site with

topics relating to IEP team membership, discipline regulations, and state and district-wide assessments. Read sample articles from the professional journal *TEACHING Exceptional Children* by clicking on the link under the tab, "CEC Publications."
http://www.ideapractices.org

References and Recommended Reading

Biklen, D. (1992). *Schooling without labels: Parents, educators, and inclusive education.* Philadelphia, PA: Temple University Press.

Duquette, C. (2001). *Students at risk: Solutions to classroom challenges.* Portland, ME: Stenhouse.

Hallahan, D., & Kauffman, J. (2005). *Exceptional learners: Introduction to special education,* 10th ed. Boston: Allyn & Bacon.

Halvorsen, A., & Neary, T. (2000). *Building inclusive schools: Tools and strategies for success.* Boston: Allyn & Bacon.

Harwell, J. (2002). *Complete learning disabilities handbook: Ready-to-use strategies & activities for teaching students with learning disabilities.* San Francisco: Jossey-Bass.

Hudak, G. (1996). A suburban tale: Representation and segregation in special needs education. In J. Kincheloe, S., Steinberg, & A. Gresson. *Measured lies: The bell curve* (pp. 315–330). New York: St. Martin's.

ldonline.org. (2005). Types of LD. Retrieved 08 July 2005 from *http://www.ldonline.org/abcs_info/ld_types.html*

Shelton, C., & Pollingue, A. (2000). *The exceptional teacher's handbook: The first-year special education teacher's guide for success.* Thousand Oaks. CA: Corwin.

Smith, T. E. C., Polloway, E., Patton, J. R., & Dowdy, C. A. (2004). *Teaching students with special needs in inclusive settings.* Boston: Allyn & Bacon.

Stainback, W., & Stainback, S. (1996). *Controversial issues confronting special education: Divergent perspectives.* Boston: Allyn & Bacon.

Swanson, H. L. (2003). *Handbook of learning disabilities.* New York: Guilford.

Physical Abilities

A Place to Begin

Every school population has students with varying degrees of physical challenges and disabilities, each with different needs. Students who are overweight have different needs from those who suffer food allergies. Those in wheelchairs need different accommodations from those who are hearing impaired. How does your school meet the needs of students who are differently abled?

Every teacher should think about and plan for meeting students' physical requirements in the classroom. We also should understand how the curriculum we teach conveys messages of inclusion and understanding about the physically disabled. For example, are there images of students in wheelchairs in the textbooks we use? Do we make references to people with disabilities in class discussions and lectures? Are the images of people on our walls and in our teaching materials representative of different body types?

One physical disability that has become more public in recent years is food allergies, the most common being an allergy to nuts. This often severe allergy has prompted many schools to ban nuts and nut products entirely from the school building. But many students also have other allergies. What precautions must be taken to ensure the safety of all students with allergies?

Look at the cartoon that begins this chapter. What do you think the children will do? How might this scene translate to a school context?

NARRATIVE 20

Before You Read

Think about the places and occasions in your school when food is present. Do you include food in your lessons? Classroom celebrations? Snack time? If so, which (if any) foods are excluded or prohibited from these activities? Why? Is it fair to exclude certain foods from your classroom because of one or two children with specific allergies? Why or why not? How do you balance the rights of the majority of students with the needs of a few?

Allergies

I grew up in an intensely diverse and very inclusive community with members from many races, cultures, ethnic groups, religions, and disabilities. However, a recent occurrence made me recall one incident of noninclusion that happened to me in third grade.

While many people think of diversity as having to do with commonly recognized differences, one difference not usually noted is food allergies. Food allergies for children can be a major issue in the classroom, both from a social standpoint and a learning one. Often teachers incorporate food into lessons—either as a material for teaching a subject, such as math or science, or as a reward for a job well done. Food is also used for celebrations including classroom birthdays and holiday festivals. Teachers who have never dealt with someone with a serious food allergy sometimes question its validity or the extent to which a child can have a reaction to certain foods.

Growing up, I had severe allergies to chocolate, nuts, milk, and milk products (cheese, yogurt, ice cream, etc). To some, this list may seem overwhelming; just hearing it has, on occasion, engendered such statements from others as, "Well, what can you eat?" Like lots of people with food allergies, I was taught at home at an early age what foods to avoid. In some ways, this made me stronger. I learned as soon as I could talk how to just say "No, thank you" even to other children and adults at friends' birthday parties who might try to coax or coerce me into ingesting something I knew I shouldn't eat. As an adolescent, this by now ingrained ability to withstand peer pressure certainly stood me in good stead; it enabled me to have the strength to say no to substance abuse and other dangerous activities some of my peers were becoming involved in.

However, as an elementary school child, sometimes my requirements excluded me from social situations surrounding food in the classroom, leaving me feeling isolated. For instance, I could not participate in the trading of snacks that was encouraged as sharing in my kindergarten class because many of my classmates' snacks contained ingredients that my body could not tolerate. If I ate something that contained nuts, for example, my throat would immediately close up; I would have severe difficulty breathing, break out in a rash, and could even go into anaphylactic shock.

Aside from kindergarten snack sharing, my food allergies didn't pose any major school problems until I hit Mrs. Snyder's classroom in third grade. On the first day of school every year, my mother would send with me a list of my allergies for the teacher. Teachers unfamiliar with how to deal with a child with severe allergies would usually contact my parents or the school nurse privately for guidance—but not this time. Mrs. Snyder decided to cross-examine me in front of the whole class on the first day of school.

The worst part about my allergies has been that, on occasion, the mere smell of substantial quantities of peanut butter or chocolate in a confined or unventilated space, even if I wasn't eating it, could be enough to cause me to have breathing difficulties. Learning this, Mrs. Snyder banned certain foods from entering her classroom at all, even if they were not to be opened and eaten there. This may seem like a good solution, but with no further explanation to the class Mrs. Snyder said something like, "Melissa can't be around certain foods so we are no longer allowing chocolate, peanut butter, and so forth to be brought to school." Failing to explain what an allergy is and naming me as the cause for banning all the major treats made some of my peers view me as, at the very least, a "spoiler" for the rest of the year.

Recently at college a similar experience happened that brought back all those feelings of being excluded and hurt and looked at as a "killjoy" and an inconvenience to the "normal" students. In one class, the instructor was presenting a lesson on classroom inclusion with a focus on ways to make all students feel like they are a member of the classroom community. To do this, she had many activities planned to demonstrate the establishment of such a community. The very first activity of the day was to read a book called *The M&M Counting Book* and then distribute M&M candies to the class so that we could mimic the activity in the book. Now, I can usually easily tolerate one or two people in the room eating chocolate. But having each member of a 30-person class eating and playing with M&Ms in the close space of our college's classrooms was just too much for me. The instructor thought that by also offering Skittles® (which contain no chocolate), she had provided a viable alternative for those who didn't like or were allergic to chocolate. However, she didn't understand that someone with a severe allergy could get sick from simply being in a room surrounded by the smell of what they are allergic to. Instead of opening up the problem to group brainstorming to find the best way as educators to include me in this activity given my allergy, the instructor sent me and my partner to another classroom to work with the Skittles®.

As we left , I felt as if all eyes were on us and I started to feel again those third-grade feelings from Mrs. Snyder's class. My partner and I went next door and worked on the activity for 25 minutes or so until the assistant instructor came in to admit that she had forgotten about us and that our class had already moved on from the M&M lesson to a different activity (which we had thus missed). At that point, any remaining feeling in me that I was part of this class community vanished. I reentered the classroom feeling like an outsider. Even as an adult, I began to feel like someone who couldn't participate the right way in a group activity. What must children in such a situation feel? Can they learn at all in such an environment, or does the fact of their physical challenge become an overriding learning block?

Unfortunately, the college class situation didn't end there. Even though the instructors had moved on to a new chocolate-free lesson, the smell from the candy still permeated the room. It immediately overwhelmed me and hives began to form on my chest and arms. My eyes began to water severely and I felt my throat tighten as I moved to my seat. Aware of my struggle, my partner alerted the instructor (interrupting her in front of the entire class) and asked her to open the windows to vent the room. It was about 55 degrees outside with a light rain; the heavy windows were shoved open and my breathing slowly began to ease, but I was painfully aware of my classmates' goosebumps and shivers. Nauseous and hurt, I left the room and went to the bathroom where I stayed for quite a while until a student finally came by to check on me. Feeling a lot more at ease and having vomited twice, I felt ready to go back to the class which still had (because this was the very first activity) more than two hours left. When I returned, I was placed in another group that was sent to work in another room because of "Melissa's allergy." Although I explained to my instructor that with the classroom vented out, I, along with my group, was perfectly capable of staying with the rest of the class, she decided to err on the side of caution. I can't say that I blame her, since, as my instructor, her first responsibility was to ensure my physical well-being, just as mine will be to my students in the near future when I have my own class.

My purpose in telling this story is to record the situation from the student's perspective. Even though, as a rational adult and teacher-in-training, I knew intellectually that my instructor was fulfilling her responsibility to protect me from potential harm, I still couldn't help feeling that to some extent I had been excluded for a second time, again taking others with me, to complete the assignment in exile. Concerned that we might be forgotten again, I returned to the original classroom periodically to peer in and make sure everyone was still working on the same activity. I regretted that my previous partner had missed part of a lesson and did not want the same thing to happen to my new group.

I didn't feel like a member of the classroom community at all that day. The instructor had, albeit inadvertently and with the best intentions, created a climate in which I didn't feel comfortable learning. When asked at the end of the day to recap what we had learned, I had nothing to report. However, on reflection I and those of my classmates who were sensitive to the learning climate on that day actually gained enormous insight. We learned that it doesn't matter by what means or methods you teach reading or math or science or social studies if you have already alienated students from their classroom learning community. We learned that a student who is not physically and emotionally comfortable cannot effectively learn. We learned that creating community is not just for the majority of students, but for all.

Our students will be diverse and have different physical abilities. We must prepare for that diversity and, when unexpectedly confronted with a challenge that we did not anticipate, we must find strategies that encourage the group to come up together as a unit with solutions for how everyone can be included. In this way, diversity becomes a strength to share, not a problem to solve.

Questions to Consider

1. Have you ever had a similar experience with a student with allergies in your classroom? What happened? How did you respond?
2. The author's third grade teacher announced to the class without explanation that the author was the reason for banning certain foods. What would you have said to the class?
3. In the college incident, what were some of the instructor's options in designing her lesson/activity? In your opinion, did she react appropriately to her students' needs?
4. The author describes feeling like a "killjoy" and a "spoiler" due to her allergy. How might her teachers have eased her guilt feelings? What might have been done to include her more in the classroom community?
5. How would you establish a classroom community? Present to your class a brief outline of the steps you would take.

NARRATIVE 21

Before You Read

Think about what training you would need to be able to work successfully with a blind student in your classroom. What questions would you have? Who would you go to for answers?

Think about all of the lessons, didactic materials, and paraphernalia in your classroom that is dependent on your students seeing them. What, if anything, in your curriculum would you have to adapt to be able to meet the needs of a blind student in your class? How might you change your class to welcome a blind student?

Spanish in Sign

When I first learned that Tamara would be in my class, I did not leap for joy. Instead, I was rather anxious. I thought, "What will I do with a blind student in my foreign language class? Language is not just learned from a book. I need visuals, maps, manipulatives!" I was concerned that I wasn't advised earlier so that I could be better prepared. I was worried about being able to accommodate this child. I needed help!

These thoughts and a multitude of questions raced through my mind. The more I contemplated what I foresaw as a problem, the more upset I became. I wasn't prepared for this in the special education component of my Master's program. Sure, I've worked with students with AD(H)D. I could do that, but this was different.

I felt like a rookie teacher, even though I had been teaching for close to a decade. I was still revising my curriculum, which was challenging enough for the sighted student. "How could I reach Tamara?" I wondered. My highly visual, graphics-dependent, interactive curriculum was designed for the sighted, and I wasn't sure how to change it. "She cannot see my visuals. She cannot see a map. How will she move around the room to participate in Total Physical Response (TPR) activities? Do I include her or do I act as if she isn't there?" I was half hoping that she wouldn't show up—so many students with disabilities opt out of language class. Maybe Tamara would do the same . . .

But there she was on the first day of class—brailled text, assistant, and all. "Well," I thought, "I'll talk with her academic teacher. She should know what to do."

Tamara's teacher gave me a list of approaches and suggestions for teaching the visually impaired, but it was all so general. She was feeling her way through this as much I was. She helped me learn to use the braille writer, but later I found out that it was not the same braille system that should be used for Spanish! I felt a sense of accomplishment when I learned to use the machine only to find that I was doing it incorrectly! How was I supposed to know that there's a different system for Spanish words? Furthermore, I wondered if Tamara knew this system well enough to be proficient in the classroom. Just think, two braille alphabet systems—English and Spanish.

I had hoped that having the workbook brailled for Tamara would have solved most of the problems, but what about the worksheets? What about maps? I was told to ask one of the school secretaries for help in brailling the worksheets. Even though I felt unqualified to help Tamara, I plugged along the best I could.

One day I realized that the map in Tamara's brailled book was not a map at all, but merely a list of the names of the South American countries in braille. Class was a few hours away, so I decided to get creative: I used wax sticks, wool, and pennies so that Tamara could tell the difference between North and South America by using various textures. I had no idea if it would work—talk about the blind leading the blind. It may be cliché, but it was so true in this case. But sure enough, it worked!

With the school term well on its way, it's still hard to anticipate what Tamara needs and what will work all the time. I've had her book and worksheets brailled. I've had her touch the different textures of realia so that she could describe them. I've had students guide her around the room during TPR activities. I have even used games, music, chants, rhythms, and instruments to involve Tamara as much as possible. Necessity has truly been the mother of invention, but I'm still not satisfied. I need continual dialogue with her academic teacher, her parents, and with Tamara herself to make this class work for her.

Tamara's participating, but only when I call on her. Her Spanish communication is limited to the classroom. How can she study and practice Spanish at home? How can I get her to communicate more proficiently? I've provided her with the vocabulary and language structures that she needs for class, but she seems so uncomfortable and unsure of herself.

Moreover, apart from the assistant and students who help her move around the room, Tamara doesn't seem to have many friends. I thought that surely my students would be more compassionate. The boys just seem to leave her alone. They tolerate her, but they haven't incorporated her into their social groups. On the other hand, one or two girls are very kind to her and go out of their way to really be a part of her experience at the school. Yet, they are the minority. The other students don't know what to do with Tamara, so they exclude her. This is disappointing and painful for me to watch.

After several months, I've noticed that Tamara is beginning to understand the language and even use it more freely, but I'm still not reaching her as deeply as I'd like. She's learning a lot of phrases, and we've even made flash cards, but where's the communication? Maybe I'm expecting too much. This is my job, and she is a normal child, her blindness aside. However, I'm frustrated because my efforts do not seem to reap great results. I feel too as if I'm all alone with this. Furthermore, I receive almost no feedback from Tamara. Despite my attempts to connect with her, I don't even know if she likes class. She doesn't ask questions. She doesn't emote. She's just there. Yes, she gets good grades, but I'd like to see the real Tamara emerge. I just want her to be like her classmates. Is that too unreasonable for me to ask? Am I that oblivious to the reality of her blindness? Could it be that what I thought was crucial in Tamara's second language experience wasn't? Could it be that the main thing in the way of my teaching her is my own sightedness?

The funniest thing happened one day. We were tossing a ball around as part of an activity, and I tossed it to Tamara. I forgot that she's blind! Thankfully she has a good sense of humor and laughed. Actually, we all did.

Now that the school term is almost over, I've taken stock of all that Tamara has accomplished in Spanish class. She can communicate her wants, needs, and opinions in basic Spanish. She knows a great deal about the geography and cultures of the Spanish-speaking world, and is ready to continue her studies next year. I hope that her next teacher realizes that it'll take more than a textbook to teach a child with physical needs. It takes compassion, ingenuity, effort, and willingness to do the unthinkable even when you don't know what the outcome will be. After a year with Tamara, I feel much more able to help students with her special needs learn Spanish, but I wish I had been this prepared back in September!

Questions to Consider

1. What are the teacher's main concerns on learning that she will be working with a blind student in her Spanish class? In your opinion, is she concerned about what's truly most important? Why or why not?

2. What do you think the narrator means when she says, "I felt like a rookie teacher even though I had been teaching for close to a decade?" What does this statement imply about how much she values classroom experience?

3. What about this teacher's Spanish curriculum makes it particularly challenging to work with Tamara? How would you solve at least one of these issues?

4. Aside from the curriculum, what other aspects of Tamara's class experience concerns the teacher? Describe Tamara's relationship with her peers. How would you encourage greater contact between Tamara and her classmates?

5. The teacher asks, "I just want her to be like her classmates. Is that too unreasonable for me to ask?" What do you think? Why?

6. The author claims to now be better prepared to help students such as Tamara. What personal qualities and abilities has she developed? How might she have made herself more ready back in September?

Project and Extension Activities

1. Some aspects of the school's physical setting may seem like torture to students. Draw a map of your classroom's layout. Now list your students' physical characteristics. Are all items in the room accessible to all students? Are students with eye problems seated in the front of the room? Are larger students seated comfortably? Redesign your floor plan to meet the physical needs of all of your students.

2. Look at this cartoon:

How do students who are overweight suffer prejudice in school? Have you observed any students in your class who struggle with their weight? Do their classmates make negative comments? Interview a student (or an adult who was overweight as a child) who struggles (or has struggled) with a weight problem. Address the following questions:
- How do you feel about your body?
- Who defines what is the perfect weight for you? How do these prescriptions make you feel?

- Have you suffered any prejudice or name calling in school due to your weight? Please describe the incident(s).
- How do your classmates' reactions to your weight make you feel?
- Does your weight affect your performance in school? If so, in what ways? If you were to design a magazine for your interviewee, what would it look like? Write a list of articles, monthly columns, and advertisements you might include in such a magazine.

3. Read this list of terms that are and are not acceptable to use when referring to individuals with physical disabilities:

Acceptable Terms	Unacceptable Terms
Person with a disability.	Cripple, cripples—the image conveyed is of a twisted, deformed, useless body.
Disability, a general term used for functional limitation that interferes with a person's ability, for example, to walk, hear or lift. It may refer to a physical, mental or sensory condition.	Handicap, handicapped person or handicapped.
People with cerebral palsy, people with spinal cord injuries.	Cerebral palsied, spinal cord injured, etc. Never identify people solely by their disability.
Person who had a spinal cord injury, polio, a stroke, etc. or a person who has multiple sclerosis, muscular dystrophy, arthritis, etc.	Victim. People with disabilities do not like to be perceived as victims for the rest of their lives, long after any victimization has occurred.
Has a disability, has a condition of (spina bifida, etc.), or born without legs, etc.	Defective, defect, deformed, vegetable. These words are offensive, dehumanizing, degrading and stigmatizing.
Deafness/hearing impairment. Deafness refers to a person who has a total loss of hearing. Hearing impairment refers to a person who has a partial loss of hearing within a range from slight to severe.	Deaf and dumb is as bad as it sounds. The inability to hear or speak does not indicate intelligence.
Hard of hearing describes a hearing-impaired person who communicates through speaking and speech-reading, and who usually has listening and hearing abilities adequate for ordinary telephone communication. Many hard of hearing individuals use a hearing aid.	

Person who has a mental or developmental disability.	Retarded, moron, imbecile, idiot. These are offensive to people who bear the label.
Use a wheelchair or crutches; a wheelchair user; walks with crutches.	Confined/restricted to a wheelchair; wheel chair bound. Most people who use a wheelchair or mobility devices do not regard them as confining. They are viewed as liberating; a means of getting around.
Able-bodied; able to walk, see, hear, etc.; people who are not disabled.	Healthy, when used to contrast with "disabled." Healthy implies that the person with a disability is unhealthy. Many people with disabilities have excellent health.
People who do not have a disability.	Normal. When used as the opposite of disabled, this implies that the person is abnormal. No one wants to be labeled as abnormal.
A person who has (name of disability.) Example: A person who has multiple sclerosis.	Afflicted with, suffers from. Most people with disabilities do not regard themselves as afflicted or suffering continually. Afflicted: a disability is not an affliction.

Source: J. Babbitt, Disability Access Office, City of San Antonio Planning. Reprinted by permission.

Do you feel comfortable with the terminology? Why or why not? Review your school's literature about physical disabilities (you may locate this information in your Guidance office or in the school literature). What terms does your school use to refer to people with physical disabilities? Are there any changes that you would make to your school's literature? If so, present a proposal to your school leadership to change the documents. Use references such as the City of San Antonio Planning website (see References and Recommended Reading) and others that you may find on the Web or from other schools.

4. Read this now-infamous quote from Jimmy "The Greek" Snyder:

"The black is the better athlete. And he practices to be the better athlete because this goes way back to the slave period. The slave owner would breed this big black with big black woman so he could have a big black kid. That's where it all started" ("Loose lips" [2001], n.p.).

What stereotypes, both positive and negative, do you know of that connect physical abilities to one's race or ethnicity? Create a list with a partner and debate each one. Think about the ways that these stereotypes affect the way you work with students in the classroom.

5. Look at the cartoons on pages 184 and 185.

Both images attempt to help the viewer to understand the world of a person with a physical disability. Create a cartoon that depicts a physical disability or challenge that you have experienced.

6. To experience firsthand the daily challenges of a physical disability, try one of the following simulations:
   • Blindfold yourself.
   • Confine yourself to a wheelchair.
   • Tie one arm behind your back.
   • Use ear plugs.

   Spend at least several hours in this simulated state of disability. If possible, spend an entire day doing this simulation. After your experience, answer the following questions:
   • How did you feel being disabled?
   • What daily tasks did you find most difficult? Why?
   • What insight did the experience give you into the challenges of being disabled?

   Design a workshop for colleagues in which you lead them through a similar simulation. After the experience, discuss your reactions in small groups.

7. Look at the cartoon at the start of this chapter. What message is the artist trying to convey with this image? Interview a person who suffers from a food allergy. Include the following questions in your interview:
   • How did you discover the fact that you were allergic to (name of food)?
   • What type of reaction do you suffer from contact with (name of food)?
   • How does this allergy affect your daily life?

Cultural Exploration

1. *Explore people:* Interview a student with a physical disability. Address the following questions in your interview:
   • What is it like to be a student in this school? Do you feel comfortable in all of your classes? Why or why not?
   • What elements of your physical disability would you want to hide in school? How does this make you feel?
   • How does your physical disability affect your academic performance? Your social interactions? Your relationship with your teachers? In what ways?
   • Was there ever an occasion when you completely forgot your physical disability in a school situation? What happened? How did you feel?
   • Did you ever experience prejudice or discrimination due to your physical disability in school? Please describe the incident.

Using the answers to these and other questions from your interview, write a brief biography of the person. Share it with your interviewee and ask for feedback as to its accuracy.

2. *Explore literature:* Choose to read about an issue regarding physical ability in schools.

Novels, Short Stories, Memoirs: choose one

- *Do You Remember the Color Blue? And Other Questions Kids Ask About Blindness,* Susan Hobart Alexander
- *Train Go Sorry,* Leah Cohen (deaf issues)
- *Deaf Like Me,* Thomas & James Spradley
- *Waist-High in the World: A Life Among the Nondisabled,* Nancy Mairs
- *Me Talk Pretty One Day,* David Sedaris

Young Adult Literature: choose two

- *Petey,* Ben Mikaelsen
- *Picking up the Pieces,* Patricia Calvert
- *Of Sound Mind,* Jean Ferris
- *The Gift of the Girl Who Could Not Hear,* Susan Schreve
- *The Weirdo,* Theodore Taylor
- *How It Feels to Live with a Physical Disability,* Jill Krementz
- *Tell Me How the Wind Sounds,* Leslie Guccione
- *The Door in the Wall,* Marguerite De Angeli

Picturebooks: Choose three

- *Paper Doll,* Elizabeth Feuer
- *Dancing Wheels,* Patricia McMahon
- *Princess Pooh,* K. M. Muldoon
- *Moses Goes to School,* Isaac Millman
- *Looking Out for Sarah,* Glenna Lang
- *Elana's Ears, or How I Became the Best Big Sister in the World,* Gloria Roth Lowell
- *Buddy's Shadow,* Shirley Becker
- *Uncle Shamus,* James Duffy
- *Handsigns: A Sign Language Alphabet,* Kathleen Fain
- *Deaf Culture: A to Z,* Walter Paul Kelly
- *The Balancing Girl,* Berniece Rabe
- *No Trouble for Grandpa,* Carol Marron
- *My Buddy,* Audrey Osofsky

Write a reaction to the literature you have chosen. Address the following questions:
- What were your thoughts about the issue before your reading?
- Did those thoughts change after your reading? If so, how?
- Did you learn anything new about the issue? What, if anything, surprised you?

3. *Explore film:* Portrayals of people with physical disabilities in film are not common. When they do appear, they may be inauthentic or even offensive. Choose one film and analyze the portrayal of a specific character. Determine whether you feel that the disability is accurately or stereotypically represented. Here are some suggestions:

> *The Best Years of Our Lives* (1946)
> *The Miracle Worker* (1962)
> *The Elephant Man* (1980)
> *Whose Life Is It Anyway?* (1981)
> *Children of a Lesser God* (1986)
> *My Left Foot* (1989)
> *Passion Fish* (1992)
> *Lorenzo's Oil* (1992)
> *The Water Dance* (1992)
> *Breaking the Waves* (1996)
> *Simon Birch* (1998)
> *The Mighty* (1998)
> *At First Sight* (1999)

Answer the following questions:
- What physical disability is this character intended to represent?
- What does the character *do* that makes her or him representative of the group?
- How does the character *look* that makes him or her representative of the group?
- In what ways is the character funny? Successful? Intelligent? What are her or his dominant characteristics?
- Do you like this character? Why or why not?

Now interview someone with the same or similar physical disability as the character (Note: your interviewee should have seen the same film and be somewhat familiar with the character). Ask the following questions:
- Is this character a valid representation of your disability? If yes, in what ways? If no, why not?
- Do you feel that this character has brought positive or negative attention to your disability? Why?
- If you were given the keys to a film studio for a day, and were able to create a movie about your disability, what would your main character be like?

Internet Connection

The Food Allergy and Anaphylaxis Network

Click on the link to "Managing Food Allergies in School," where you can sign your school up for a free food allergy program for elementary, intermediate, and high schools—a multimedia program that includes an educational video, an EpiPen trainer, a poster, and a binder with over 100 pages of information and standardized forms. You can also download a "Food Allergy Action Plan" for your school.
http://www.foodallergy.org

World Association of Persons with Disabilities

An excellent resource for information about assistive devices. Contains an extensive list of links to specific disabilities. There is a collection of personal stories about living with disabilities as well.
http://www.wapd.org

American Disability Association

This site includes a list with biographies of great Americans with disabilities as well as information about civil rights cases. Of particular interest are the links to Americans with Disabilities Act (ADA) and to ADA Compliance Guidelines and Standards.
http://www.adanet.org

Disability Museum

This site includes a fully searchable library with text and graphics resources as well as a virtual museum. Click on the "Education" link for teacher resources and course packets.
http://www.disabilitymuseum.org/

The American Federation for the Blind

When you first arrive at the homepage, try the "Change Colors and Text Size" link to view alternate versions of the website. Under "Learn about," click on "Education," where you will find links to teacher resources and Individuals with Disabilities Education Act (IDEA) information. There is also a great "Solutions Forum" for teachers and other professionals.
http://www.afb.org

Alexander Graham Bell Association for the Deaf and Hard of Hearing

Click on the "Professionals" tab to visit the Public School Caucus or sign up to receive email action alerts. The site contains a wealth of information about hearing loss and a list of periodicals and other relevant publications.
http://www.agbell.org

References and Recommended Reading

Bigge, J. L., Best, S. J., & Wolff Heller, K. (2001). *Teaching individuals with physical, health, or multiple disabilities,* 4th ed. Upper Saddle River, NJ: Merrill/Prentice Hall.

Block, M. E. (2000). *A teacher's guide to including students with disabilities in general physical education.* Baltimore, MD: Brookes.

Disability Access Office. (n.d.). *Disability etiquette handbook.* San Antonio, TX: City of San Antonio Planning. Retrieved 24 June 2005 from *http://www.sanantonio.gov/planning/disability_handbook/deh12.asp*

Cornwall, J., & Robertson, C. (1998). *IEPs—Physical disabilities and medical conditions (Individual Education Plans).* London: David Fulton.

Haskell, S. H. (1993). *The education of children with physical and neurological disabilities.* London: Nelson Thornes.

Heller, K. W., Forney, P. E., Alberto, P. A., Schwartzman, M. N., & Goeckel, T. (2000). *Meeting physical and health needs of children with disabilities: Teaching student participation and management.* Belmont, CA: Wadsworth.

Imber, M., & van Geel, T. (2005). *A teacher's guide to education law.* Mahwah, NJ: Lawrence Erlbaum Associates.

Loose ships sink ships . . . and political careers too. (2002). *Detroit News,* 18 December. Retrieved from *http://www.detnews.com/2002/homelife/0212/19/d01-38371.htm*

Norden, M. (1994). *The cinema of isolation: A history of physical disability in the movies.* Piscataway, NJ: Rutgers University Press.

Index